COSTUME DESIGN
THE BASICS

Costume Design: The Basics provides an overview of the fundamental principles of theatrical costume design, from pre-production through opening night.

Beginning with a discussion of what costume design is, why people wear clothes, and what the role of the costume designer is, this book makes accessible the art and practice of costume design. Peppered with interviews with working costume designers, it provides an understanding of what it means to be a costume designer and offers a strong foundation for additional study.

Readers will learn:

- How to use clues from the script to decipher a character's wardrobe
- Methods used to sketch ideas using traditional or digital media
- How to discuss a concept with a team of directors, producers, and designers
- Strategies to use when collaborating with a professional costume shop
- How to maintain a healthy work/life balance
- Courses of action when working under a limited money and labor budget.

Costume Design: The Basics is an ideal starting point for aspiring designers looking for ways to achieve the best costumes on stage and realize their vision into a visual story told through clothing.

T. M. Delligatti is a Service Assistant Professor of Costuming at West Virginia University and has constructed over a hundred shows professionally at Shakespeare & Company, Hartford Stage, Connecticut Repertory Theatre, and many others.

THE BASICS

The Basics is a highly successful series of accessible guidebooks which provide an overview of the fundamental principles of a subject area in a jargon-free and undaunting format.

Intended for students approaching a subject for the first time, the books both introduce the essentials of a subject and provide an ideal springboard for further study. With over 50 titles spanning subjects from artificial intelligence (AI) to women's studies, *The Basics* are an ideal starting point for students seeking to understand a subject area.

Each text comes with recommendations for further study and gradually introduces the complexities and nuances within a subject.

SPECIAL EDUCATIONAL NEEDS AND DISABILITY (THIRD EDITION)
JANICE WEARMOUTH

SPORT MANAGEMENT
ROBERT WILSON AND MARK PIEKARZ

SPORTS COACHING
LAURA PURDY

TRANSLATION
JULIANE HOUSE

TOWN PLANNING
TONY HALL

WOMEN'S STUDIES (SECOND EDITION)
BONNIE G. SMITH

SIGMUND FREUD
JANET SAYERS

COSTUME DESIGN
T. M. DELLIGATTI

For a full list of titles in this series, please visit:
www.routledge.com/The-Basics/book-series/B

COSTUME DESIGN

THE BASICS

T. M. Delligatti

Routledge
Taylor & Francis Group

NEW YORK AND LONDON

First published 2021
by Routledge
52 Vanderbilt Avenue, New York, NY 10017

and by Routledge
2 Park Square, Milton Park, Abingdon, Oxon OX14 4RN

Routledge is an imprint of the Taylor & Francis Group, an informa business

© 2021 Taylor & Francis

The right of T. M. Delligatti to be identified as author of this work
has been asserted by them in accordance with sections 77 and 78
of the Copyright, Designs and Patents Act 1988.

Library of Congress Cataloging-in-Publication Data
Names: Delligatti, T. M., author.
Title: Costume design : the basics / T.M. Delligatti.
Description: New York, NY : Routledge, 2021. |
Series: The basics |
Includes bibliographical references and index.
Identifiers: LCCN 2020015258 (print) | LCCN 2020015259 (ebook) |
ISBN 9780367374174 (hardback) | ISBN 9780367374181 (paperback) |
ISBN 9780429354304 (ebook)
Subjects: LCSH: Costume design.
Classification: LCC PN2067 .D45 2021 (print) |
LCC PN2067 (ebook) | DDC 792.02/6–dc23
LC record available at https://lccn.loc.gov/2020015258
LC ebook record available at https://lccn.loc.gov/2020015259

ISBN: 978-0-367-37417-4 (hbk)
ISBN: 978-0-367-37418-1 (pbk)
ISBN: 978-0-429-35430-4 (ebk)

Typeset in Bembo
by Newgen Publishing UK

CV 12.16.2022 1242

For my parents, Gary and Carol Delligatti

CONTENTS

FIGURES

ACKNOWLEDGMENTS

To those who've aided me on this journey: Janice Ferger, Katie McCarthy, Casey McNamara, Emily Stafford, Cody Lorich, Lauren Brennan, Ambrose Hall, Hugh Blackthorne, Cecily Steinhour, Tonia Markou, Feren White, and Joanna Koefoed.

INTRODUCTION

INTRODUCTION

The first rule of costume design is *there are no rules*, but there are guidelines and conventions that can increase chances of success, helping the new costume designer develop an eye for what is effective. But what does it mean to be "effective"? How do designers know when their work is "good"?

Costumes are garments that bring a character to life. They tell a story of a person, of a creature in the night, of a monster, a whimsical spirit, and countless others. Using clothes as context clues, the audience can know a character's personality before they say a single word. They help immerse an audience in a story and make them suspend their disbelief for a few short hours. Costume design creates **verisimilitude**—a show that is *verisimilitudinous* means its world feels plausible enough to be believable to an audience. It is the illusion of reality.

The best designer's work looks effortless on stage, as if the characters in the play are real people and not actors. What a layperson does not see is the thousands of hours of research, drawing, planning, discussion, shopping, building, and improvising. The script offers words for the actor, but costume designers—in collaboration with scenic, light, and sound—put the character into the world.

A designer wields two main tools: an understanding of human behavior and the costume itself (which can include clothing, masks, makeup, and a variety of accessories). When designers read a script, they must figure out the core of each character's personality. After a thorough knowledge is gained, they dress characters in a way that makes that character believable within the world the team wants to create.

In order to understand a character enough to choose their wardrobe, first, a designer must understand why people wear clothes.

WHY PEOPLE WEAR CLOTHES

In 3300 BCE, a 45-year-old man died on the Ötztal Alps, his body soon frozen within the glacier. In 1991, two hikers discovered his perfectly preserved body, including his clothing. Scientists named him Ötzi.

Ötzi wore a grass cloak, a sheep-hide loincloth, and a coat sewn together with pieces of goat and sheep fur. The shoes had been carefully constructed with deer hide using dry grass as insulation. With this outfit, Ötzi could face the profound cold, the torrential winds, the heavy rains, and all the deep snow that came with living in the mountains.

Just like with Ötzi, clothes helped humans survive the earliest stages of civilization, but even our ancestors did not use clothing only for protection. Clothing evolved to represent a symbol of culture and expressions and humans imbued countless personal meanings to fabrics, shapes, colors, lines, and textures. Ötzi was only one of many discoveries that revealed the behaviors of early humans.

Humans developed ways to use our clothing to project our wants, needs, moods, and personalities to ourselves and the people around us. The section below addresses individual categories, but often the reasons for wearing clothes overlap with many categories. A garment can both serve as protection from the cold and be an artistic statement. It can protect against the cold and act as an expression of identity. Clothing is a nuanced art form, one that constantly evolves.

Time of Year, Time of Day

Big wool coats are for chilly weather, like a winter stroll through the woods, while flip flops are for braving the summer heat. Not only do people wear different clothes based on the seasonal weather, but fashionable colors and fabrics change with the time of year as well.

Spring might bring brighter colors and patterns that pop. Winter garments are heftier and often sport darker, earthier tones.

Dress also varies depending on the time of day. For nights, a person could curl up on the couch in comfy pajamas. For mornings, a college student might don the only clean hoodie to make an 8 AM class. In certain times in history, an aristocrat might have an entirely different outfit for afternoon tea or dinner.

Ceremony and Tradition

Academic robes and mortarboards have become the modern symbol of graduation. For a wedding ceremony in western culture, white dresses and black tuxedos have become so ingrained since Britain's Queen Victoria married in white, it has become a cultural standard.

Religion

People wear clothes specific to their faith. Some wear their clothes for piety, some as a show of their morals, and some for ritual. Catholic priests wear an *Alb*, a stole, and a *chasuble* during mass. Jewish people wear *yarmulkes* as a sign of devoutness. Shinto and Buddhist priests wear *Jōe* to rituals.

Profession

Jobs in an office may have dress codes, called *business attire*, requiring their employees to wear garments that represent the company's mission. Often, this comes in the form of suits, ties, collared blouses, and knee length skirts. Painters or builders have messy jobs, needing clothing made of durable fabrics that can get dirty. A police officer's uniform signals their role in upholding the law. Hazmat suits protect workers from toxic environments. In the theater, a stage crew is required to wear all black so that they don't attract the audience's attention.

To Show Belonging to a Particular Group

Cliques, gangs, clubs, and groups of like-minded people dress similarly to be identified as a single unit. They use accessories, shirts, colors, or patterns to prove they represent a singular identity. Kids at a summer camp can wear matching shirts. In medieval Europe, heraldry showed loyalty to a family heritage. March bands use their uniforms to appear as a singular unit.

Military

On the battlefield, uniforms help soldiers tell friend from foe. Outside of battle, a uniform's style, color, stripes, and medals can identify a soldier's rank, country, military branch, and length of service.

Sports and Recreation

Like the military, a uniform for a sports team helps fans and fellow players identify who is who on the field. Numbers on uniforms help the crowd pick out individual players. The chess club may have special hats they wear to competitions. Non-competitive sports also need specific styles of clothes to help athletes achieve their goals. Scaling Mount Everest, for example, would be even more of a challenge without crampons, a snowsuit, and an oxygen tank.

Gender Expression

Cultures throughout history have assigned masculine and feminine values onto specific garments. In some societies, pink, fluffy gowns represent the essence of femininity, while sharply tailored suits in dark colors illustrate an idea of manhood. Dresses, cowboy boots, crowns, and tiaras all bring to mind degrees of masculinity and femininity. These can be worn straight to express a "pure" form of gender (as defined by individual cultures) or they can be combined in numerous ways to create androgynous looks that bridge between masculine, feminine, and non-binary.

Culture

Textures, prints, patterns, and silhouettes have evolved in all corners of the world. Tartan is traditionally associated with Scotland. A kimono conjures the image of Japanese culture. Styles from around the world can migrate across the world and influence the fashions of nations.

Sometimes it happens peacefully through trade. Sometimes it's not so peaceful, forced through war and colonization.

Modesty

Social conventions dictate which parts of the human body should be covered in polite company. How much of the body is covered depends on the era, the country, the social class, along with the personal feelings of the wearer themselves.

When researching, it's good to know these broad reasons, but studying individuals can bring nuance to a design. People wear clothes for more reasons than can be accounted for in a single book. A designer can extrapolate much about a person's personality, identity, temperament, and disposition from interviews about a person's wardrobe choices. This is what costume design as a discipline seeks to capture on stage or on screen.

I asked a group of college students in a costume history class why they chose the outfit they were wearing. Answers ranged from, *it was comfy*, *it was the only thing clean*, and *I have an interview later*. These details give small clues into a person. I asked the same survey to a broader audience, with answers solicited from social media:

> So, appropriate attire: oxblood Doc Martens, faded and torn black Moto jeans, oxblood t-shirt, light cabled black woolen hat I knit, because it's spring and cool in the shade. Boxer briefs, Diesel.
>
> I bought these things because they're comfy and I like them? And I don't know where my Docs are from the 90s, so I bought these a few years ago. Style and foot support. I've had these all for a while except the hat, which I made lately. Wool from a local shop. Jeans and t-shirt from H&M. Boxers because comfort.
>
> (Hugh Blackthorne)

> Powder blue sleeveless shift dress. Pink and purple oriental flower pattern. Baby blue Mary Jane heels—think 50s wedding—with white tips, leather bows and gold heart clasps. Translucent pink crisscross choker, my signature pink flower hair clip. Fuchsia bikini bottoms with lace hips, purplish gray bra with a tiny bow

between the breasts. Hidden skin tone nylon socks. Fashion is my first passion, so I only wear dresses and ridiculously girly shoes.

I always look for the most unique and feminine clothes to stand out and express myself. Yet I pride myself on finding phenomenal deals. My shoes were $31 including shipping because they're from China and my dress was severely clearanced at Kohl's so only $11.

(Paige Johnson)

Red, black, and white (mostly red) bikini bottoms and a black triangle bikini top. Light-wash denim cutoff shorts with a high waist. A cream cropped singlet with a few buttons at the front. Brown Havaianas. Brown and purple sunglasses and a black Roxy cap (just realised I'm wearing a whole lot of Roxy today)

I bought most of it online rather than in store. Reasons—first of all, it was on sale. The bikini I liked the cut and colour of the bottom (red is my favourite colour) and there was no top on sale that matched so I went with plain black, especially since they had a simple triangle top without all the frills. I'm long waisted so I try to buy high waisted shorts and shorter tops because they suit me better. I also tend towards lighter denim and colours like cream because they suit my skin tone. Havaianas, I have a lot, but brown goes with most of my clothes so they're my favourite. The cap was a gift and the sunglasses were one of the few pairs that don't look ridiculous on me. So, I guess you could say I've carefully crafted this 'I don't care too much' look, lol.

(Amy Ward-Smith)

A designer can imagine many combinations of personalities that fit the interviewee's clothing choices above, but they must always remember that people are nuanced. Producing an effective costume design means understanding the complexities of human nature.

Characters are a representation of real people. Designers use what they know about people to portray a character the audience will believe. Shakespeare's scripts are a great place to start practicing the creation of character through clothing because his scripts are dense and can be interpreted in numerous ways. Romeo from Shakespeare's *Romeo and Juliet* is a young man in love with the idea of being in love.

Hamlet, from Shakespeare's *The Tragedy of Hamlet, Prince of Denmark*, is a man who has grown suspicious and bitter after the death of his father. Just by the nature of their personalities, their outfits should be designed differently, even if both shows are set in the same time period.

Hamlet is a closed off and defensive character. His costumes are usually dark, precise, and constricted. Romeo waxes philosophically about love. His costumes tend to be more open, lighter, rebellious, and freer.

If a designer switched the looks, Romeo may come off more ironic and sneering than he is. Hamlet could come off as more fickle and more frivolous. Why? Because of the way people interpret color and line. Dark clothing may be equated with dourness, which feels different to an audience than the way romantic heroes are typically portrayed. Bright, light, and open costumes feel lively and carefree, which contrasts Hamlet's mourning of his father. Whatever choice is made must come from a deep understanding of the character, the clothing, and the overall vision of the team.

A designer could devise a character who is a bookish, introverted type with glasses (to show that constant reading strains the eyes) and ill-fitting clothes (to show the character is too absorbed in their studies to worry about appearance). Muted colors might say a person doesn't like to stand out. This interpretation plays into the classic nerdy type. It is a way for the audience to know the basics of the character before they do or say anything on stage.

A designer can make a different kind of statement by breaking the audience's expectation. This is called **subversion**. The same bookish, introverted character from the previous example could be dressed in bright, attention-grabbing colors in an eccentric style. This demonstrates a different personality even though the text didn't change. Every choice a costume designer makes says something different.

THE COSTUME DESIGNER'S PROCESS: WHAT TO EXPECT

The following gives a basic overview of the costume designer's process from hiring to the end of their contract. Once the general order of events is established, the subsequent chapters will break down each section in detail.

Reading the Script

The first task for a designer is to study the script and form basic ideas about the characters and the setting. Who are the characters and what are their personalities? What are the characters' social and economic class? What is the time period of the play? Where is the play set geographically? What are the play's unifying ideas? What is the playwright trying to say to the audience? Are specific events mentioned in the script like proms, weddings, masquerades, or other ceremonies? The answers to these questions will create a foundation that a costume design can be built upon.

Along with a character analysis, the designer will then notate information such as the number of costume changes for each character and document the scenes they appear in. Once a script is thoroughly scoured for wardrobe clues and hints, the next step is research.

To illustrate how a designer might break down a text, this book will use examples from Shakespeare, specifically *Much Ado About Nothing*, to talk about the script analysis process. The reader does not need to know the play to understand the example, but a familiarity will give the reader some context to the analysis section of Chapter 1.

Researching the Play's Context and Exploring Themes

The context around a play's settings gives insight into its **themes**, which is a topic that is repeatedly explored within a story. Love, redemption, and justice are themes commonly encountered in literature. Knowing a playwright's intent is not always possible nor is it necessarily needed, but a designer can infer through research the original meaning, or they can use alternative interpretations of the text and create their own meaning.

For example, stage or film adaptation of H. G. Wells's *War of the Worlds*, originally published in 1870, could use the author's themes as stated in the text. This story about an alien invasion is an exploration into Britain's fears about being colonized just as they had done to other cultures.

> And before we judge them too harshly, we must remember what ruthless and utter destruction our own species has wrought, not only upon animals, such as the vanished bison and the dodo, but

upon its inferior races … Are we such apostles of mercy as to complain if the Martians warred in the same spirit?

(From chapter 1, "The Eve of the War")

The designer can design with the author's intent in mind, or they can make note of other meanings. Some artists like to take old texts and tie them into topical events. Both are good to note as reference for conversation and research. With all these ideas compiled together, the designer will next discuss them with the director.

Meeting the Director and the Design Team

During the first meeting, the costume designer, the director, and other designers discuss the show's **concept**, which is a show's mood, tone, setting, and aesthetic. Plays that emulate real life and are about real-life situations often require a realistic concept. For example, Arthur Miller's *All My Sons* features a story loosely based on true events, set just after the end of World War II. Generally, the show's concept is portrayed with a naturalistic aesthetic, making the stage feel as lifelike as possible. Exaggerated concepts that go beyond the real can work, but going too far may distract from the play's themes. For plays with more ambiguous settings, there is more room to play with the concept. Unlike *All My Sons*, Shakespeare's *The Tempest* could easily be set on the moon, on a mountain, or in a fantasy world, for it is not the specific setting that is necessary to the story, but the idea of being stranded in a magical place far from home.

These ideas will be discussed between the designers and the director until they determine the concept that will satisfy their artistic needs and resonate with the audience they intend to present it to. Once all these ideas are debated and weighed, the director will make a final decision. The next step is research and rendering.

Another Round of Research

Once a concept is chosen, research can become more specific. For a show dependent on realism and naturalism, a designer should aim for accuracy. Audience members will know if military uniforms are wrong for the period, or if the **silhouette** of a dress is inauthentic.

They may not be able to express exactly what is wrong, but an audience is good at vocalizing when something *feels* wrong.

If the show is not set in a historical period, precise research still provides the resources needed to design. A designer can visit a museum to study **extant garments**, which are real garments from history that have survived the test of time. (All clothes before the twentieth century were made from natural fibers, which succumbs easily to rotting. The further back in time one goes, the fewer extant garments).

Photographs of everyday people are a reliable source for convincing characters, supplemented with magazine spreads and fashion photos for a little designer flair. Film or fine art styles can also be introduced in addition to period. A director might want to replicate genres such as Italian cinema, cyberpunk, or German expressionism.

Sketches and Rendering

The drawing phase is where all the ideas, research, concepts, and genres come together. The designer takes everything learned from research and discussions and begins to quickly sketch plans of what each character looks like. These sketches can be black and white with color swatches added to communicate an intended palette. The team discusses these ideas and shares critiques. Depending on the project, there could be hundreds of revisions before a consensus is reached. Once the director is happy with the sketches, the designer creates **costume renderings**. A **costume rendering** is a fully-colored illustration of each character accompanied by fabric swatches and detail drawings. The designer will render their ideas using a medium of their choosing—watercolor, digital painting, 3D modeling, and many other methods—to present the final designs to the team.

Production

With the drawing phase complete, the production phase begins with the designer presenting their drawings to the costume shop. This team will use the designer's rendering to build the garments. Drapers, stitchers, craftsman, shoppers, and managers come together to pattern, cut, build, and fit every single costume on every single actor.

The actors discover their own interpretation of the characters during rehearsal. They may have new insights into their characters that the designer never considered. The actor portraying Romeo may find a unique angle to his character that could enhance the aesthetic. A designer doesn't have to take every actor's suggestion, but it helps to listen and keep the collaborative channels open. An actor's ideas can be brilliant, giving a costume more dimensions. To dismiss them without consideration can be missing a vital opportunity.

Flexibility is important during this stage. Sometimes the design as originally rendered doesn't allow for everything an actor needs to do. The director and the designer must work together on solutions, altering as needed to maintain the intended vision.

Dress and Tech Rehearsal

Costumes are nothing without context. In tech rehearsals, everything finally comes together—scenic, lighting, sound, projections, actors, dancers, and orchestra. Designers can add their detailed adjustments one final time.

Opening Night

This is the night everyone waits for, the culmination of everyone's hard work. Even in small theaters, hundreds of people have come together to make a show happen. They celebrate as the mind turns to new projects and new adventures.

These are the fundamental elements of costume design—what it is and how it all works together.

SUMMARY

- Costume design is the art of creating character through wardrobe.
- Creating character requires an understanding of human nature and the countless reasons they wear clothing.
- A costume designer achieves their vision through a process of research, collaboration, and production.

1

TEXT ANALYSIS AND RESEARCH

The foundation of all theater, film, and television is the story. Every choice a costume designer makes is in service to it. Those stories come in many forms. Authors can pen scripts; the stories can be improvised; or they can be devised by actors, designers, writers, choreographers, and artists all together. Whichever form a story takes, a costume designer must know it intimately, for designers give color and life to the words. Theater, film, and television are about the experience of being immersed in a world that evokes thought and emotion. Each person that works on these projects contributes a piece of that world that is brought together to create a story for other people to enjoy. It is why this art form is labeled as collaborative. In order to do good work, a costume designer must understand how stories affect an audience's emotions.

The best place to begin is to dive into a script and figure out what makes characters interesting. There are many different ways a story is structured; not all of them have a concrete beginning, middle, and end. Some are told in a more abstract way, focusing on themes and movement rather than plot. The following sections will explore four types of storytelling a costume designer will commonly interact with: **Scripts**, **improvisation**, **devised theater**, and **dance**.

HOW TO READ A SCRIPT

When working in commercial theater, most plays will be produced from a script, usually written by an individual or a team. When the designers are hired, they are given that script to read and analyze before the meetings begin.

A common practice for costume designers is to read the script no less than three times—once for entertainment, once to make notes on themes and ideas, and once to think in practical terms of the production.

The first reading is for the designer's own enjoyment. The idea is that it lets the designer experience the story as a whole. In this read, the designer can make notes about how the story makes them feel (Example: "It's a somber play. The whole story has a deep sense of melancholy"), about what they think of the characters and their choices ("The main character never seemed to learn from his mistakes, which is why the play ended in tragedy"), and what the story tries to say to the audience ("The play is a cautionary tale about the dangers of isolating yourself from your friends and family"). These feelings give a designer a sense of the mood and tone of both the play and the characters.

First reads also give the designer a sense of the perspective and how the audience will experience the story when they watch the show. The design team may read a show dozens of times and watch it a dozen more over the course of a production, causing that initial emotional reaction to diminish. After so many reads, jokes may not seem funny anymore. The surprise twist may seem too obvious. As a consequence, the designer might try to rework the show to feel new again. Remembering that first read will remind the designer what the show is supposed to feel like.

The second reading requires an analytical approach to the text. The goal is to fully understand the characters and how they fit into the story. It's also beneficial to know the work's intent, meaning, and **themes**. A theme is a message the storyteller wants to communicate.

In Gabrielle-Suzanne Barbot de Villeneuve's 1740 book *La Belle et la Bête* (translated in English as *Beauty and the Beast*) one of the themes is inner beauty opposing the outward appearance of a monster. The character Beauty learns to love the Beast in spite of his grotesque appearance. In Molière's *Tartuffe*, the theme of hypocrisy is highlighted by titular character, Tartuffe. Tartuffe is a man who professes purity and other religious values, but his actions are motivated by greed and lust.

New designers and students may wonder how themes of a story are relevant to costume design if the setting and the characters are already known. Using themes can give a design a sense of sincerity.

When people consume a piece of fiction in any form—books, theater, movies, video games, TV shows—they bring with them a tolerance level for which they are able to accept unrealistic, exaggerated, or surreal elements. This is called **suspension of disbelief**. Storytellers and designers must convince a crowd to believe in monsters, ghosts, true love, or complicated murder plots. How does a designer do that through costumes?

Authenticity

Costumes need to feel authentic to the world they inhabit. Audiences can be made to accept the surreal if the world feels like it could logically exist within the rules set up by the story. For example, a sword-and-sorcery fantasy may have dragons and magic, but it's world is usually grounded in something real. In this case, these stories often utilize variations on a medieval aesthetic. Too much deviation from that aesthetic could feel out of place, breaking immersion. The costumes must feel like the characters in the world can believably buy, make, or use the clothing they wear. How much is too much deviation, though? That line is not always clear. Returning to the core themes reveals what's most important to a story, which can act as a designer's guide: *What is the story about? Will this choice support it?*

REVEALING CHARACTER THROUGH COSTUME

To illustrate how the same type of character can be designed in different ways to portray different themes and ideas, the following will look at various characterizations of a doctor character.

The Shakespeare play *Macbeth* has a doctor character in a minor role. A design is possible with this limited information—depending on the period when the show is set, a costume designer can dress the character in typical doctor garb and be done with it, but the costume design can go further with characterization. While reading the script, the designer should make notes about other characterization clues and how that might affect the costume.

Breaking down the script during the read-through can reveal volumes about the inner workings of a character: What kind of doctor is this character? Surgeon? OB-GYN? Pediatrician? This can change the style of coat, color of the scrubs, or what tools the doctor carries. In *Macbeth*, the character is Macbeth's personal physician in charge of treating Lady Macbeth as she descends into madness. How old is the doctor? How much experience do they have? What is their general personality? This can change the style and cut of the hair, what accessories the doctor wears, whether they have tattoos, wear a smartwatch, wear stilettos, and so on. What country is the doctor from? Where is the story set? Lab coats can vary in cut and color by country; sometimes, no lab coat is worn at all. What is the time period? A doctor in seventeenth-century Italy could wear a plague mask and a long robe while a nineteenth-century doctor in the United States might wear only an apron over their daywear. During the read-through, the designer can notate these questions which will act as a reference point during the research phase.

These questions add some depth, but the designer can go even deeper. The next step is to consider the character's motivation and intent: How does the story identify the characters? What is the author trying to say about their actions? What role does the character play in the story?

In another show with a doctor, the doctor's actions may be painted as misguided, clever, or as the result of hubris, such as Dr. Jekyll in Robert Louis Stevenson's *The Strange Case of Dr. Jekyll and Mr. Hyde*. The character's role in the story could be that of a cautionary tale to others. Or the doctor could be portrayed as devoted, concerned, and inquisitive, as in the previously mentioned doctor from *Macbeth*. A designer can use the color, shape, line, and texture of a costume to reinforce these ideas present in the script. This will make the character feel more fleshed out.

The following describes a basic foundation of how a change in costume can alter the way a character is perceived. The images shown in Figure 1.1 both show a "doctor," but both are characterized on two ends of a spectrum. The characters are the same in that they both serve the same role (that of a doctor), but the details are what make them distinct individuals.

The image on the left communicates a character that is messy or careless, with intentions that might not be the purest. An audience doesn't associate excessive blood stains with a conscientious doctor, even if it happens in real life. The image on the right shows a doctor who could be clean and fastidious. Or it could denote arrogance. The head wrap indicates a possible region of birth or a religion that the

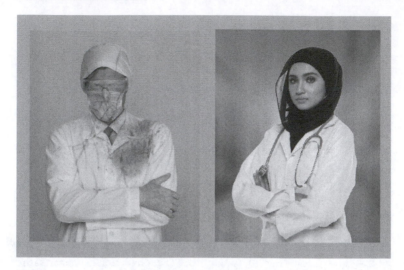

Figure 1.1 An image of two theoretical doctor characters, dressed according to specific traits and personalities.

doctor practices. Clothing choices change the nature of a character; learning the inner and outer particulars will produce a strong design. Exploring broad characters can be good practice for beginners. Over time, a designer can explore subtler techniques to create more nuanced characters.

Finally, after the designer thoroughly understands the script in-and-out, top-to-bottom, it is time for the third read-through. Scripts can be so dense that it requires multiple reads to catch everything. Subtle lines of dialogue may not seem related to costuming initially but could be crucial to the design. Take a line like, "I play the violin every evening in the symphony." It might seem like this is more an interesting bit of characterization than something that directly affects costumes, but someone who knows the violin will know that this character needs natural, functional nails. Violins can only be effectively played with short nails. If this line is overlooked and the designer dresses this character in an evening gown with nails to match, the actor won't be able to believably play the role.

The third read-through is also the time to create the necessary paperwork and plan out any practical concerns that arise. The costume plot is created in this phase, which will be addressed in detail in the next chapter. If characters need to change costumes in quick succession, this is the time to make note so the designer can integrate any solutions into the design at the start.

A FURTHER STUDY INTO THEMES

To break down a story and find the themes, one can start with the broad, general questions: Is the show a comedy, tragedy, mystery, musical, or other genre? What are the setting and the time period? Who are the characters?

As an example, the following is a break down of Agatha Christie's *The Mousetrap*:

> Genre: Mousetrap is a whodunit mystery
> Setting: Mid–20th century England in a bed and breakfast during a snowstorm.
> Characters: The lead characters are Mollie Ralston, the lady of the house; Giles Ralston, her husband, etc.

The above facts set a foundation. The next layer is to research the context of the story—did historical events influence the story? Many plays are written with some kind of historical grounding even if the events in the show are fantastical. Sometimes, an author's personal history colors the plot.

The Mousetrap *is based on the real-life case of Dennis O'Neill, a young Welsh boy who was killed at the hands of his foster parents in 1945.*

Next is to look for a subject the story revolves around. What subject is the story addressing?

In The Mousetrap*, many characters are affected by childhood neglect, either indirectly or directly, and they all deal with the consequences in their own ways. Some ignore the role they played in the neglect and some are so deeply hurt by it that they've vowed to take revenge.*

A common theme of many Whodunit mysteries is that of judging people by their outward appearance, and *The Mousetrap* is no exception. When the murder happens, it is up to the audience and the characters to figure out which character is the murderer.

In terms of costuming, these themes can be communicated in a few ways. The characters' feelings of guilt might mean they dress more conservatively as a way to close themselves off. This could mean a blouse that is high-necked or a dress that is rigid enough to restrict free movement. A character that has pushed aside guilt and grasped onto a sense of righteousness might dress showier as a way to flaunt their authority with designer watches, flashy jewelry, expensive-looking haircuts, and finely tailored suits that show off wealth.

Paratext

Another useful tool to research during the second read is a story's **paratext**, which is supplemental material provided by publishers, editors, or the author themselves in order to give direction or clarify the text. Blurbs, forewords, footnotes, and asides are the traditional sources of paratext, each giving the script different perspectives and interpretations. They're useful for older plays like Shakespeare or Greek tragedies because they can explain references lost to history. Tweets, author blogs, and social media posts are also part of the paratext.

While paratext can give a story a frame of reference, it doesn't need to be followed precisely. Sometimes an author or publisher can augment their story with facts shared on blogs or social media—they might tweet that they always believed the protagonist in their story had green hair and purple teeth, or that their villain should wear overalls—but a designer doesn't need to follow this paratext unless it gives information that is necessary to understanding the plot, characters, or theme.

Paratext is useful when it reinforces the meaning of the text or adds clarity to something that would otherwise be ambiguous. Arbitrarily changing the hair and teeth color of a character may not add much to the story and characterization, but something like a change in casting would.

Cloud Nine by Caryl Churchill (1979) is a play about gender and racial roles in the UK, set in both Victorian Africa and in London, 1979. In the introduction, Caryl Churchill suggests a specific casting for the characters.

> When I came to write the play, I returned to an idea that had been touched on briefly in the workshop—the parallel between

colonial and sexual oppression, which Genet calls 'the colonial or feminine mentality of interiorised repression'. So the first act of Cloud Nine takes place in Victorian Africa, where Clive, the white man, imposes his ideals on his family and the natives. Betty, Clive's wife, is played by a man because she wants to be what men want her to be, and, in the same way, Joshua, the black servant, is played by a white man because he wants to be what whites want him to be. Betty does not value herself as a woman, nor does Joshua value himself as a black. Edward, Clive's son, is played by a woman for a different reason partly to do with the stage convention of having boys played by women (Peter Pan, radio plays, etc.) and partly with highlighting the way Clive tries to impose traditional male behaviour on him. Clive struggles throughout the act to maintain the world he wants to see—a faithful wife, a manly son … It is essential for Joshua to be played by a white, Betty (I) by a man, Edward (I) by a woman, and Cathy by a man.[1]

Because the play makes statements on gender roles in society, disregarding the paratext in this case would change the show's premise and actively work against the themes.

Subtext

Subtext is a hidden meaning underneath the action and dialogue. Some clues for the costume can be hidden in the script's subtext. To find subtext, a designer must look beyond the words said by a character and their literal meaning.

When looking to see how subtext can be used to enhance a story, detective mysteries are a good place to start. Mysteries are stories where subtext is the primary feature. The genre is designed for readers to look beneath the dialogue to find clues to solve the mystery. Characters often don't say what they mean. The story leaves deliberate holes for the audience to deduce the solution along with the characters.

Subtext doesn't have to come directly from the script; the costume designer, in collaboration with sets, lighting, and sound, can insert their own subtext into a scene.

The following exchange shows how a designer can take basic dialogue and include subtext in a scene with simple costume choices.

> JAMAL: "How are you doing?"
> SIOBHAN: "I'm fine."

With a literal reading, Jamal wants to know how Siobhan is feeling. Siobhan responds that she's doing well. Now, add some context:

> <JAMAL enters a room and finds a dozen cans of cheap beer scattered on the floor>
> JAMAL: "How are you doing?"
> <SIOBHAN, her clothes and hair disheveled, curls around the bowl of a toilet>
> SIOBHAN: "I'm fine."

With the small number of added clues in the stage direction, the subtext of this scene shifts from the literal definition of the words spoken, to the implied meaning that Jamal may not be asking the question out of politeness but out of concern, and Siobhan is, in fact, not fine at all.

Let's change the context again, altering some costume pieces:

> <JAMAL enters the room. He's dressed in a t-shirt and old jeans that are soaked in blood.>
> JAMAL: "How are you doing?"
> <SIOBHAN smooths out her suit pants then puts her hair up in an immaculate bun>
> SIOBHAN: "I'm fine."

This scene is not as clear as the previous examples and can be interpreted in many ways. Perhaps Jamal protected Siobhan from an attacker, and came into the room to check if she was okay. Or maybe Siobhan ordered a hit that Jamal carried out.

Subtext is further added when actors bring their own interpretation of a scene. Every artist's contribution to the story is linked with the other artists, including the costume designer. Interpretations transform as the process progresses, and adaptation to that change is what makes a well-rounded costume design.

Metaphor

Metaphors in stories can provide deep insights into character, if they are decoded. With metaphor, an artist uses symbols or figurative language to represent an idea. It is a comparison devised to articulate a point and is not meant to be taken literally.

> Nadheer is a star.
> Sofia's mind is an encyclopedia.

A costume designer wouldn't dress Nadheer as a star blazing in the sky, nor would Sofia need an encyclopedia hat. Both are metaphors, with Nadheer's sentence representing his fame and Sofia's representing her knowledge. It reveals a hint of their characterization, which costume designers can utilize in determining their personality and wardrobe.

Metaphors can also be utilized beyond sentence level. Entire stories are written not to be taken as literal truth, but as an example of a message the author wants to portray. Fairy tales and fables are the quintessential story-as-metaphor. In the story *The Frog Prince* by the Brothers Grimm, a princess is handsomely rewarded for allowing a frog to eat from her table and share her bed. The story is a metaphor, imparting to readers the moral values of keeping your promises. In an adaptation of these fables, a costume designer has the choice to portray these characters as they are literally written—a frog and a princess—or play on the figurative meaning of what they represent. As an example, the frog character can be dressed as a downtrodden man in need of someone to help him. Perhaps this could be something like a rumpled suit the character had slept in. The princess can be portrayed as a woman of high privilege who has the means and the resources to help others. This costume could be a fashionable dress with expensive accessories. This is just one interpretation of these characters. Modifying the interpretation can reshape the entire meaning of the text. If a designer reversed the characterization and made the princess character the one who is destitute, and the frog the character with wealth, it shifts the power dynamic between the characters, changing the meaning of the story just with a difference in wardrobe. In this scenario, no longer does the princess learn to keep her promises with those she considers below her station. She becomes a character that is taken advantage of by a person in a more powerful position.

Shakespeare makes extensive use of complicated metaphors, all of which can inform wardrobe choices, the color palette, and texture of the costumes. In Sonnet 18, Shakespeare compares a lover to summer.

> Shall I compare thee to a summer's day?
> Thou art more lovely and more temperate:
> Rough winds do shake the darling buds of May,
> And summer's lease hath all too short a date;
> Sometime too hot the eye of heaven shines,
> And often is his gold complexion dimm'd;
> And every fair from fair sometime declines,
> By chance or nature's changing course untrimm'd;
> But thy eternal summer shall not fade,
> Nor lose possession of that fair thou ow'st;
> Nor shall death brag thou wander'st in his shade,
> When in eternal lines to time thou grow'st:
> So long as men can breathe or eyes can see,
> So long lives this, and this gives life to thee.

The metaphorical imagery here is rich for a designer. The speaker of this sonnet compares the subject to summer, but then points out summer's flaws: "Too hot," "too short," "rough winds," "Shadowed by clouds." The summer imagery evokes a variety of possible colors a designer could use: golds, reds, browns, oranges, peaches, and verdant greens. For the style of costume, "hot," "short," "rough," and "shadowed" can create a most alluring attire that matches the intensity of the sonnet.

Framing

Human beings are creatures of emotion, which is the driving force behind art. Rare is a story that is emotionally neutral about a subject, and the ones that do exist may feel like a news story rather than a gripping drama. Audiences respond to emotion. We want them to cry, laugh, cheer, or wish for the characters to get their comeuppance.

A costume designer can use their craft to frame a story or characters around the desired emotions. It's all about manipulating the visuals to elicit an audience response—if something is funny, you want the audience to laugh. If something is sad, you want the audience to cry. The way to achieve this is through framing.

Superhero stories are an excellent entry point for beginners to decode how the story frames ideas. The villains are framed as unquestionably bad, wanting to destroy the world, rule the world, or steal lots of money and power. The heroes want to preserve the world and save people's lives. The people who have created this kind of story want the audience to feel that "destroying the world is bad" and "saving civilian lives is good." When the heroes nearly fail, the audience feels suspense, wondering if they can succeed. When the villain is defeated, the audience feels excitement, relief, pride, or joy. The villains are dressed in dark colors and sharp lines. This has been ingrained in the public consciousness as having a specific meaning, that of "evil" or "amoral." The heroes are in brighter colors and softer lines, which the audience associates with heroism. This is called **shorthand**, when an artist (or in this case, a costume designer) uses imagery an audience will recognize to convey information. This is the most basic kind of framing.

Costume designers can play with the framing—perhaps they switch the color schemes, making the protagonists dark and the antagonists light. With this change, the audience might interpret the main characters as anti-heroes or rebels, bad boys and girls who don't play by society's rules. This change in interpretation can happen even if the script doesn't change at all. That is how costume design can affect framing.

Complex framing comes from designs that either pass no judgment on the character or judgment is subtle. Some stories have no clear heroes and villains. The characters can represent people dealing with the circumstances they are given, for better or for worse. Subtly framed costumes give off a vibe but don't explicitly show an opinion. This often allows the audience to ponder in the visuals as presented to them so that they may pass their own judgment.

Romeo and Juliet is a story where the framing can depend on the design team. Some think *Romeo and Juliet* is framed as a cautionary tale—had the families not been fighting, their children might still be alive. Others think it's a romantic tale about true love conquering all even in death. Some think it's both. Whichever interpretation is used, the design can fortify the message.

Is such a thorough script breakdown always needed? In an ideal world, it should be done every time, but a designer's contract might not allow for the time to do an exhaustive study. However, the more widely read and experienced a designer is, the easier the process gets.

As a designer, there is no need to format the analysis as if it were an academic paper. It can be notes jotted down on paper or files saved in a folder on a computer. It can be kept informal, but it should be organized so information can be readily found. If the notes need referenced during the design process, the answer could be found in the notes, but it is only useful if those notes are easy to search through. A **dramaturg** may also want to write a school study guide about the costumes and may need to know what the costumes symbolize in relation to the story. For student designers, the notes are pivotal to a writing project for a capstone or thesis. In short, organizational skills are best developed early on, for they will be crucial in the later stages of designing a show.

THEATER WITHOUT FORMAL SCRIPTS

Improvisation

With improvisational theater, there is no text to analyze. Actors react to prompts according to the situation, sometimes guided by the audience. Examining the characters may seem difficult if the story changes every night. Improv shows are built on a framework, usually in the form of a pre-existing premise the performers augment in rehearsal. Some have a bare-bones script the actors use to lead them during the performance. At the start of the process, enough information should exist to get the costume designer started with the surface components. Then, they should talk with the actors about their ideas and attend as many rehearsals as possible.

For example, a designer could be hired to costume a stage or TV adaptation of the Dead Author's Podcast, a 2011 show co-produced by The Time Travel Mart and Lucky Bird Media, was an improv podcast performed in front of a live studio audience. The program took the form of a late-night talk show, hosted by Paul F. Thompkins playing English writer H. G. Wells. He interviewed classic dead authors, like J. R. R. Tolkien and Plato, played by various guest comedians, using pre-prepared questions and Twitter questions submitted by the audience.

To begin analysis, the designer could begin by answering the following three questions:

- What is the setting of the show? *It's a talk show.*
- What are the personalities of the characters being portrayed? *They're based on real historical figures whose personalities are exaggerated for comedic effect.*
- What is the tone of the show? *It is comedy/satire/parody.*

Without a set script, the designer can turn to the actors to help them with analysis. Attending rehearsals and observing the actors can help determine the style of humor. If the actor is going for a more realistic interpretation, as actor Jessica Chaffin did playing Agatha Christie, the designer may want to support it with a natural-looking costume. The humor would come from the situation rather than exist as a sight gag.

However, a sight gag might be the best way to emphasize comedy like slapstick. Actor Jason Mantzoukas portrayed Greek philosopher Plato as a modern frat boy, making full use of crude expletives to comedic effect; this contrasts with the audience expectation that the philosopher would carry himself in a dignified manner and use formal speech. A designer can reinforce the crude presentation by giving this version of Plato a revealing costume more fitting for a toga party than ancient Greece. Or, a designer could dress him with anachronistic accessories like a smartwatch, making him visually analogous to the style of comedy.

In improv, the costumes must ebb and flow with the nature of the actors and their characters.

Devised Theater

Devised theater is a collaborative work where the story is created with a team, usually through workshops and rehearsals. Costume designers can be involved in this process and influence the direction of the story, or they can come in after the script is complete.

If it's the latter, the script analysis works the same as a normal script with the advantage that the authors may be accessible for questions or open to changes, clarifying any ambiguity in the text.

If it's the former, designers can use their expertise and aesthetic sense to shape the story as it's being written.

Dance

Dance may not have a traditional script, but it is plentiful with themes. The music, lyrics, and movement are what communicates the story. Sometimes, the story is told in a concrete way, with the movements of dance playing out like a silent film; sometimes, it's abstract. Either way, a designer's job does not change. The costumes must support the story.

To become familiar with the expected genre conventions, a designer can watch many different kinds of performances and note the movement and which part of the body needs to be emphasized. Dancers usually have specific costume needs to meet both their range of motion and their desired aesthetics. There is reason ballet dancers aren't in large, unwieldy gowns and ice dancers in skirts that train. Clothing must be chosen that is both appropriate for the needs of the performer and aesthetically appropriate for the theme.

If a designer can't attend performances in their local area, some libraries stock archival footage. The New York Public Library's Jerome Robbins Dance Division documents thousands of videos and moving images of past dance performances. YouTube can also be an invaluable resource as long as caution is exercised (red flags to look for will be explored in the upcoming chapter on using the internet for research).

PRACTICING A SCRIPT ANALYSIS: SHAKESPEARE'S *MUCH ADO ABOUT NOTHING*

The following is an abridged practical exercise in analyzing a script for costumes using Shakespeare's *Much Ado About Nothing*. The goal of this one way a costume designer can approach the text and build a foundation for research. It will be more about the ideas the costumes will communicate—it won't be direct costume ideas like, "Beatrice will wear a halter dress with stiletto heels," but more about inter-pretation and meaning, i.e., "Beatrice should look formal but playful, dressed to impress no one but herself." We'll look briefly at two sets of characters: Beatrice and Benedick, the main couple, and Hero and Claudio, the secondary couple.

The Analysis

Much Ado About Nothing is categorized as one of Shakespeare's comedies, which communicates to a designer that the general tone of the design might be lighthearted and frivolous, with plentiful amounts of melodrama.

Paratext

The title is a play on words. Taken literally, it describes a situation where people fret over trivial things—"making mountains out of molehills" as the common idiom says. In Shakespeare's time "Nothing" was also vulgar slang used when Shakespeare's characters are being indecent about women. This means the play title can also be interpreted as "Much fuss over women's naughty bits," which is the central conflict of the play: The love interest, named Claudio, is tricked into believing his betrothed, Hero, is not a virgin. The title of *Much Ado* clues audiences in to the style of the show, which makes use of comedic wordplay and is not afraid of a little bawdiness.

With this context, a risqué or playful costume design could fit into Shakespeare's intent. A designer could use this to play around with the social mores around modesty versus sensuality and what that means in this society. In the play, the villain, Don Jon, sets to ruin the main characters by soiling Hero's image of purity. The costume designer can either reinforce or subvert this theme depending on what costume is chosen for her. A humble, demure outfit might emphasize her dedication to virginity and follows the role society has given her. If Hero's outfit were racier, it might imply that this standard of chastity is more imposed upon her rather than something she adopts. Both are legitimate interpretations of the character; the ultimate decision on her design would depend on how the designer wants to portray them.

Theme

The central theme is deception, both the useful kind and the harmful kind. The play doesn't depict lying as being inherently problematic. In fact, it portrays deceit as being helpful in some situations. The main characters lie to each other as a way for them to see the truth. Characters are always wearing masks of some kind. They wear actual masks from a party scene early in the play and figurative masks to hide parts of themselves that they don't want others to see. This is where much of the play's conflicts come from. The character Benedick tries to hide the fact that he's a hopeless romantic by loudly proclaiming to others that he disdains the idea of marriage. Hero must fake her own death as a way to protect herself when she is falsely accused of infidelity. This means a designer must determine whether to dress these characters as their true selves or dress them as they project themselves. Should Benedick look like a hopeless romantic? Or should he look cocky? When Hero is proven innocent, should she be dressed looser and freer, or should she be returned to the symbol of modesty and purity she was always meant to be?

Framing

Hero and Claudio, one of the show's two romantic couples, closely follow traditional western romantic conventions, representing the pure, virginal wealthy woman and the heroic, courageous soldier who desires to win her heart.

For Hero, the script reveals very little about her actual appearance. Most of the dialogue that describes her is filtered through characters that either idolize her, insult her, or slander her.

> Claudio: Is she not a modest young lady?
> …
> Benedick: Why, i'faith, methinks she's too low for high praise, too brown for fair praise, and too little for great praise. Only this commendation I can afford her, that were she other than she is, she were unhandsome, and being no other but as she is, I do not like her.
> Claudio: Thou thinkest I am in sport. I pray thee tell me truly how thou lik'st her.
> Benedick: Would you buy her, that you enquire after her?
> Claudio: Can the world buy such a jewel?
> Benedick: Yea, and a case to put it into. But speak you this with a sad brow? Or do you play the flouting jack, to tell us Cupid is a good hare-finder and Vulcan a rare carpenter? Come, in what key shall a man take you to go in the song?

Claudio: In mine eyes she is the sweetest lady that ever I looked on.

In this scene, the script is framing Hero through two conflicting views. Claudio, sick with puppy love, thinks she is the most beautiful woman in the world. Benedick, who has sworn off all women (and who might be suppressing his love for Beatrice), thinks she is common and hardly worth any kind of praise. The truth probably lies in the middle of each of their opinions. However, costumes can shift audience sympathy toward either character's viewpoint depending on the choices. Dressing Hero to look stunningly gorgeous like a model will make Benedick look more arrogant and petty (not necessarily a bad choice on how to portray him, since his behavior is juvenile in the opening scenes). Claudio may end up looking superficial. The audience might question if he likes Hero for Hero, or if he likes her looks and status. Romantic heroines are commonly dressed to look beautiful, with the expectation that the audience will want the "princess" to be with her perfect "knight." But this play deconstructs that trope when the older, bickering couple steals the spotlight. If the designer follows the trope and makes Hero beautiful, it will support this reading.

Hero doesn't have to be dressed that way; she could be plain or maybe even a little dowdy, which would bring out an idealistic, naive quality in Claudio, but Benedick may end up sounding churlish and rude. This is the core of framing: How does the designer want the audience to perceive these characters?

Metaphor

The *Much Ado* script utilizes many metaphors to describe the characters. One such metaphor is at the beginning when Claudio is introduced by a messenger.

Messenger: Much deserved on his part, and equally remembered by Don Pedro. He hath borne himself beyond the promise of his age, doing in the figure of a lamb the feats of a lion. He hath better bettered expectation than you must expect of me to tell you how.

"Doing in the figure of a lamb the feats of a lion" is a metaphor for Claudio's youth and his skillfulness in battle. In costuming, it could mean that he excelled in battle in spite of his small build. It might not mean anything about his body type and just be about his youth. A designer could dress him in a suit that makes him look large and intimidating, which would contrast with his youthful idealism. The possibilities of what he could be number many, but what he shouldn't be is mature because that would contradict what this metaphor says about his nature.

This was a small sampling of one type of analysis a costume designer can do to prepare for a design, but there are many ways to go about it. Reading, practice, and experience help a designer develop their own methods that work for their style of design.

SUMMARY

- A costume designer's first tool is the script; it is the source for the design.
- Design is in service to the story. The choices made for the production can elevate the script.
- To analyze a script for costumes, a designer must know the plot, characters, and themes.
- Improvisation, devised theater, and dance are other types of design without a traditional script, but a similar analytical approach can be utilized in these forms as well.

NOTE

1 The excerpt from the introduction to *Cloud 9* by Caryl Churchill is copyright ©1983 Caryl Churchill Limited, reprinted with permission of Nick Hern Books. *www.nickhernbooks.co.uk*

2

BEGINNING THE DESIGN PROCESS

EARLY PAPERWORK

Organization and paperwork are far from the most creative aspect of a designer's job. For that reason, students and new designers may choose to skip it in favor of "the fun stuff." However, it is the designer's organization that maximizes the efficiency of the afore-mentioned "fun stuff." Early pre-production paperwork helps the designer anticipate challenges and keeps the later processes running smoothly. It lays the groundwork for the upcoming costume build. When in conversations with the design team, good paperwork allows costume designers to make informed choices.

The costume plot is the first piece of paperwork a designer will make, created as they read the script.

What Is a Costume Plot?

The costume plot is a guide that tracks how many costumes are in the show, when they are worn, and how many times an actor or character must change outfits. Some musicals have dozens of cast members playing hundreds of roles, many on stage for only seconds at a time. The costume plot is a way to organize all actors and costume changes into scenes.

A costume plot is usually started during the script analysis phase, even if the show isn't cast yet. Parts of the document will change once a director decides the actor's roles, but the initial estimation is enough to begin the process of research and budgeting.

Once the costume designer has software they like, the next step is to create a table. The top row contains all the show's scenes. Should a script have no designated scenes, the chart can be divided into French scenes, which segments the text into blocks based on when an actor enters or leaves the stage. A stage manager may already have a list of French scenes for the designer to use.

When first plotting during the script analysis phase, the first column will list all the characters. Eventually, when the show is cast, the designer can add the actors' names. If the director does not know how many actors are needed to fill the chorus, the number can be estimated based on chorus sizes from the past in similar shows. It is better to overestimate a cast size rather than underestimate. Chorus members can be shifted around or added during the rehearsal process; if a designer underestimated the number, they might have to rush order a costume, using up the budget. Changes will happen; a designer needs to be flexible and update the paperwork as often as needed.

Once the table is made, the designer goes through the script page by page and marks which character is present in each scene, making a brief notation about the costumes they wear, i.e., "prom gown," "tuxedo," "casual." Some designers like to color-code costume changes to gain a visual understanding of the scope of the show. Figure 2.1 shows what a simple play may look like and Figure 2.2 shows what a musical could look like.

For film, several versions of the costume plot may need to exist depending on who is using it. Film plots may have information about the filming locations or shooting schedule. Because the extras in a film can have upwards of 400 people, they may need their own costume plot separated by scene and set location.

The amount of detail in the costume plot depends on the designer's needs. Some may like a simple sheet for easy reference. Some may want a comprehensive list of all the individual pieces of clothing an actor will wear. There is no "correct" strategy, only one that helps the designer and the costume team meet their goals. A new designer should experiment with different types of plots to see which one meshes best with their design style.

The plot serves multiple purposes. First, it is used to estimate the total number of costumes needed. If a play has eight lead characters with five costume changes and a chorus of ten actors with seven changes marked on the plot, a designer knows the show will need 110 total costumes.

						Romeo and Juliet Costume Plot						
Character	Act I Prologue	Act I Scene 1	I.2	1.3	1.4	1.5 2. Prologue	2.1	2.2	2.3	2.4	2.5	2.6
Escalus		Royal wear										
Paris			In gown									
Lord Montague		Basic 1										
Lord Capulet		Basic 1	In gown									Wedding
Romeo		Basic 1	Street wear	Ball/ Mask	Ball/ Mask		Ball/ Mask	Ball/ Mask	Unkempt	Basic 2		
Mercutio		Basic 1		Ball/ Mask	Ball/ Mask		Ball/ Mask			Basic 1		
Benvolio		Basic 1	Street wear	Ball/ Mask	Ball/ Mask		Ball/ Mask			Basic 2		
Tybalt		Basic 1		Ball/ Mask	Ball/ Mask							
Friar Laurence	Friar					Friar			Friar			Friar
Friar John					Ball/ Mask							
Balthasar		Street wear/ Armed			Ball/ Mask							
Sampson		Street wear/ Armed			Ball/ Mask							
Peter		Street wear/ Armed			Ball/ Mask					Basic 1	Basic 1	
Abraham		Street wear/ Armed			Ball/ Mask							
An Apothecary		Street wear/ Armed			Ball/ Mask							
Old Man		Street wear/ Armed			Ball/ Mask							

Figure 2.1 A sample costume plot for a production of Shakespeare's Romeo and Juliet.

Character						
Musician 1	Street wear/ Armed		Musician			
Musician 2	Street wear/ Armed		Musician			
Musician 3	Street wear/ Armed		Musician			
Page 1	Street wear/ Armed		Ball/ Mask			
Page 2	Street wear/ Armed		Ball/ Mask			
Lady Montague	Basic 1					
Lady Capulet	Basic 1	Basic 1	Ball/ Mask	Nightgown	Basic 2	
Juliet		Basic 1	Ball/ Mask			Wedding
Nurse		Nurse	Nurse	Nurse	Nurse	
Gregory	Street wear/ Armed		Ball/ Mask			
Citizen	Street wear/ Armed		Ball/ Mask			
Servant	Servant		Servant/ Ball			
Servant 2	Street wear/ Armed	Servant				
Servant 3	Street wear/ Armed		Servant/ Ball			

Figure 2.1 Continued

	Scene 1.1 "Overture"	Scene 1.2 "Welcome to Town"	Scene 1.3 "I Want a Thing"	Scene 1.4 "Going on an adventure"	Scene 1.5 "Stumbling Block"	Scene 1.6 "From Reaction to Action"	Scene 1.7 "Romance is like Flowers"	Scene 1.8 "All is Lost"	Scene 2.1 "The Hero Fights"	Scene 2.2 "A Winner is Me"
The Protagonist	Base Streetwear		Ballgown	Ballgown minus Shawl	Climbing Gear	Add: Crampons	Same	Remove: Hat	Business Suit	Sparkly gown
The Love Interest	Base Streetwear		Ballgown		Climbing Gear	Add: Crampons	Same	Add: Blood	Hospital Gown	Sparkly gown
The Mentor	Old Man	Add: Satchel		Old Man	Climbing Gear	Add: Crampons			Shopkeeper	Dance outfit
The Friend	Base Streetwear		Ballgown	Tuxedo	Climbing Gear	Add: Crampons		Remove: Hat	Casual	Sparkly gown
The Rival	Base Streetwear	Add: Hat	Tuxedo	Tuxedo	Climbing Gear	Add: Crampons	Same	Pilot uniform	Business Suit	Dance outfit
The Other Love Interest	Ball Gown		Tuxedo		Friday Casual		Same		Business Suit	Dance outfit
Animal Friend	Bear Suit		Bear Suit	Bear Suit	Bear Suit				Bear suit	Bear Suit
Henchman 1	Base Thug	Add: Hat	Bear Suit	Base Thug		Business Suit		Flight attendant	Business Suit	Dance outfit
Henchman 2	Base Thug	Add: Hat				Business Suit		Flight attendant	Business Suit	Dance outfit
Henchman 3	Base Thug	Add: Hat				Business Suit		Flight attendant	Nurse Uniform	Dance outfit
Dancer 1	Base Streetwear	Add: Parasol					Tutu			Sparkly gown
Dancer 2	Base Streetwear	Add: Parasol					Ballet			Sparkly gown
Chorus 1	Base Streetwear	Add: Parasol	Ballgown		Climbing Gear	Add: Crampons		Rescue outfit	Doctor	Dance outfit
Chorus 2	Base Streetwear	Add: Parasol	Ballgown		Climbing Gear	Add: Crampons		Rescue outfit	Nurse Uniform	Dance outfit
Chorus 3	Base Streetwear	Add: Parasol	Ballgown		Climbing Gear	Add: Crampons		Rescue outfit	Surgeon	Dance outfit
Chorus 4	Base Streetwear	Add: Parasol	Tuxedo		Climbing Gear	Add: Crampons		Paramedic	Surgeon	Dance outfit
Chorus 5	Base Streetwear	Add: Parasol	Tuxedo		Climbing Gear	Add: Crampons		Paramedic	Nurse Uniform	Dance outfit
Servant 1	Base Streetwear	Add: Parasol	Maid		Hot Dog Vendor	Same			Angel	Dance outfit
Servant 2	Base Streetwear	Add: Parasol	Maid		Janitor	Same			Angel	Dance outfit
Servant 3	Base Streetwear	Add: Parasol	Butler		Janitor	Same			Angel	Dance outfit
Servant 4	Base Streetwear	Add: Parasol	Valet		Climbing Gear	Add: Crampons				Dance outfit
Musician 1	Base Streetwear	Add: Parasol	Tuxedo		Climbing Gear		Tuxedo			Sparkly gown
Musician 2	Base Streetwear	Add: Parasol	Tuxedo		Climbing Gear		Tuxedo			Sparkly gown
Musician 3	Base Streetwear	Add: Parasol	Tuxedo		Climbing Gear		Tuxedo			Sparkly gown

Figure 2.2   A sample costume plot for a theoretical musical.

With this number, the designer can budget the show and estimate labor. For example, if the costume budget is $2000, and one hundred costumes in the plot, that means the designer can spend roughly $20 per costume. This information shows what the designer can realistically accomplish. With a budget of $20 per costume, it would not be feasible to expect silks and wools with real crystals embossed in the fabric. But if a designer needs those items to achieve what the script requires, the costume plot can be used to negotiate a higher budget.

The director may want to take advantage of the information as well. Actors may need to double—or triple-up—on roles if the chorus is large and the cast is small. With the costume plot, the director and the designer can make casting decisions based on the number of changes. Instead of having one actor change costumes a dozen times while another never changes at all, a director may want to even out the roles to relieve the first actor's burden. These situations aren't always avoidable, but collaboration can help minimize unnecessary changes.

If the double- and triple-role casting can't be adjusted, planning for these practical issues in the design phase will help a production run smoother during technical rehearsals.

Exploring Software

Before computers, designers created much of the paperwork by hand, but the digital era brought a variety of software that expedites the process and improves the ability to share the document with others. Software-created forms are also easy to read and can be made searchable. Some important software programs for a designer to learn are Microsoft Word, Microsoft Excel, Microsoft Access, Google Docs, Google Sheets, and Apple Pages.

Google Docs is a program that specializes in collaboration. Anyone with a Google account can share the plot with their assistants, the director, and the costume shop manager, all of whom can make tweaks and suggestions as needed. Google Docs is a compilation of programs that includes Google Sheets (for making spreadsheets), Google Slides (for making slideshow presentations), and Google Forms (for making polls and surveys). The biggest advantage of the Google collection is that it is free to use, but it lacks the diversity of features of other paid software programs.

Microsoft Word or Excel has a clean user interface and is easy to sync across all devices. It isn't free like Google Sheets, but it has a plethora of features that might only be available as third-party add-ons in Google.

Free Open-source programs are also available such as OpenOffice and LibreOffice. The most significant points to consider when choosing software is user friendliness and easy sharing with colleagues. When exporting, make sure all members of the team can open the file on their devices.

COLLABORATION AND THE FIRST DESIGN MEETINGS

Visual entertainment is a collaborative art. Many creative minds work together to create a singular piece of art, emphasizing the common idiom "two heads are better than one."

Costume designers make up one part of a team that can range from dozens in a small theater to thousands in a Hollywood movie. Many of those people may never meet the designer directly, but all are affected by the decisions a costume designer makes. A set decorator will need to know how the costumes fit in the scene. A 3D modeler must accurately render the outfit to look like the actual garment. An animator must make the fabric move believably. A marketer may want photographs of the actors in costume for promotional posters. The machine moves in many ways, each one vital to the others' operation. A misstep can cause problems in many areas. Cohesion is the goal, which is achieved through teamwork.

The first time all the designers, directors, and stage managers will come together is in the initial design meeting. During this meeting, the team will share their general thoughts on the story and discuss any important considerations.

The team will also discuss a show's aesthetic and style. If the script doesn't already dictate the time period and artistic approach, anything can inspire the look of the show, from 1940s Italian cinema to Victorian-era naturalism, to Japanese anime. In design, there are few limits, but the ideas chosen should be something that augments the story.

The designer should also begin a discussion if the play requires odd costumes (like a mascot suit, stilts, or extreme body padding) or special effects (like blood packs or squibs). A director will need to know what is feasible so that he or she can plan rehearsal strategies. For example, a script might call for a puppet that an actor will need for practice in rehearsal, or a story might require quick-changes that need to be integrated into the choreography.

A team that works well together produces good shows, but sometimes ideas clash. One designer's interpretation of a script can be different from another's, but the production demands that the team reach a consensus. Interpersonal communication skills mitigate conflicts before they escalate. If a problem does intensify, agreeing on compromises can save a floundering production, but they aren't always obvious. Learning how each person works and thinks can reveal solutions. A designer should encourage a discussion but shouldn't get defensive if the director gives them notes. Flexibility is crucial. One mustn't get too emotionally close to an idea. A designer may find themselves making cuts for the greater good of the production.

After the first meeting, when the concept is settled on, the designer continues their research.

RESEARCHING IDEAS

After the first design meeting, the concept is set. Perhaps the team decided to set Shakespeare's *Much Ado About Nothing* in the gilded age of Newport, Rhode Island. Maybe they wanted a more surreal approach, conceptualizing the story in a fantasy realm with magic and monsters. Whichever direction the group chooses to go, finding information about that concept is the next step.

Research can be divided into three categories: **Primary, secondary**, and **tertiary**.

Documents that record a firsthand account about a moment in history is **primary research**. This research encompasses diaries, letters, extant garments, and photographs. A photograph of a wedding in the 1940s is considered a primary resource because it shows an event as it was lived. A modern-day blog about that same wedding is not primary research because it looks back on that event and interprets it through a modern lens. It is not a lived experience, but a translation of a lived experience.

Primary research is most useful for historically set productions. Jane Austen's *Pride and Prejudice* or Chekhov's *Three Sisters* both require realistic depictions of their era because the setting intertwines with the story. Primary research provides the most accurate information about the real garments worn by people who lived in the period.

Any document, blog, or article that interprets, analyzes, or summarizes an experience is classified as **secondary research**. Secondary research is work that explains primary research materials and is usually written after the period. Fashion history blogs, encyclopedias, and textbooks all qualify as secondary research.

The following images illustrate how primary research and secondary research can work together when pursuing historical accuracy.

The photograph in Figure 2.3 shows a piece of a dress circa 2017s. It would be considered primary research, but—just like when ancient

Figure 2.3 A remnant of a prom dress. These kinds of pieces may be all historical fashion researchers have left to understand the clothing of the past.

artifacts are discovered—the information is incomplete. One might be able to deduce the general shape and type of fabric, but more clues are needed. As an experiment, without looking at Figure 2.4, try to figure out what the dress might have looked like whole using both research materials and personal memory. The second image, Figure 2.4, features what the garment actually looked like. If one had tried the experiment, note the differences between the interpretation and the reality.

The details between the experiment and the actual garment are likely different. This is secondary research: the interpreter had to use what they know to guess what the garment could've been. Secondary research can be reliable, but it should be cross-referenced with a primary resource to confirm it. In this situation, a designer can

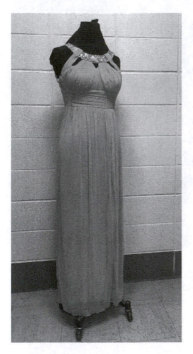

Figure 2.4 The remnant pictured in Figure 2.3 came from this 2017 prom dress.

find other similar extant garments and use those to fill in the missing information.

Sometimes primary research does not exist. Documentation could've been lost, or the era wasn't well documented in the first place. Garments made before the twentieth century were made entirely of natural fibers, which rot away. Experts in archaeology and sociology use their skills to figure out how the garment looked. In these cases, secondary research may be the only resource.

Another benefit to secondary research is that it gives context to a garment that only hindsight could've revealed. For example, Scheele's green was a popular color for dresses, wallpaper, and paints in the nineteenth century. However, the green dye was made with an arsenic compound that could cause sickness at best, death at worst. People did not know about the color's toxicity at the time, so the only clue in primary research would be letters describing suffering and illness. It wasn't just garments, though—Scheele's green was used on curtains and bedspreads. The correlation between the color and the illness wasn't discovered until later. In this case, primary and secondary research together reveals facts a designer can use. Consider a character in a Victorian-set play that is sickly and weak. Knowing this detail, the designer might dress this character in bright, vivid green, adding a sense of depth that is both informative and foreboding.

The next level is tertiary research, which is a collection of primary and secondary research. Bibliographies, almanacs, Wikipedia, and some textbooks are types of tertiary research. Tertiary sources act as a roadmap, guiding readers to the appropriate source. A designer might not want to rely on websites like Wikipedia as the only source for their research. However, Wikipedia is useful for its links to secondary sources which in turn link to primary resources. Tertiary sources are good places to find decent articles, books, and links.

RESEARCH STRATEGIES

For a Show with a Realistic Historical Setting

A costume designer has three main sources for fashion history information: museums, the library, and the Internet.

Museums house portraiture, extant garments, and textiles. Each is a primary source. Portraits may show exquisite detail on extravagant gowns and doublets. More abstract paintings may have less detail, but they communicate color, energy, and emotion, all valuable for when a designer is trying to convey a character.

There are two key considerations when using historical paintings for research. Portraits are excellent sources for characters of a noble class, but not for middle or low-class families. Paintings were expensive, with full-body paintings only affordable to the wealthiest. Jean Sorabella said in the Metropolitan Museum of Art article "Portraiture in Renaissance and Baroque Europe," that the most expensive option (the full-length portrait) expresses power and self-possession. If designing middle-class characters, a designer may need to consider a simpler version of those extravagant outfits. For peasants, merchants, and laborers, portraits may not exist. Some landscape artists painted everyday life like Jan Van Goyen's *Peasants Resting Before an Inn* in the early 1640s.

Portrait artists might've also tweaked proportions and smoothed unflattering lines to make the subject look more attractive, not unlike modern photo-editing software. Unless a designer is working a historical reenactment piece where an acute attention to detail is the point, edited paintings are acceptable to use for a costume designer's purposes. The designer would need to be aware that the garment's proportions may not resemble the painting precisely as rendered, just as with heavily-edited photographs in magazine spreads.

Artwork can be accessed through physical, print, and digital means. Visiting the museum will give a designer the truest sense of the color, detail, and scale, but it is the least accessible option. Some museums catalog their art collections in books and sell them online. These books can be easily obtained, but the printing process distorts some detail and color. Some museums photograph their collection for online browsing with 360 views and the ability to zoom in and out as needed.

Los Angeles County Museum of Art in the United States (lacma. org), the Victoria and Albert Museum in the UK (vam.ac.uk), and the National Museums of Japan (emuseum.jp) are only three of thousands of institutions that offer online catalogs of their collections. Google has partnered with dozens of museums from around the world, hosting many organizations on one convenient page (artsandculture. google.com). Many local museums will also have websites. If they don't and a designer has a particular portrait they'd like to see, the museum may be open to sending detailed photographs over e-mail.

However, like the printing process, the actual colors of a painting can be distorted on monitors.

Museums will also house collections of extant garments. Unlike portraits, where artists beautify real life by minimizing a person's flaws, extant garments show the true proportions (with "true" meaning that a person in real life wore the outfit. Their natural body shape may have been altered by corsets, undergarments, and padding). With the museum's permission, a designer can look inside to study the interior structure, feel the texture and weight of the fabric, and see its luster under lighting. Should it not be possible to look inside the garment due to its fragility, the museum might have archived photographs that can be accessed. The book *17th Century Women's Dress Patterns*, edited by Jenny Tiramani and Susan North, presents X-ray photographs of extant dresses, allowing a view of the inside previously only possible if one deconstructed the garment.

Extant garments rot over time. For some periods in history, the only evidence left behind is scraps of cloth historians have carefully pieced together. Sometimes it is just a piece of a sleeve or fragments of a shoe. In these cases, a designer can reference paintings and drawings to get an idea of what the garment might have looked like when it was whole.

Apart from the museum, a designer can turn to books, magazines, and newspapers for research. When searching for books, a designer can start with two main categories: costume history and art history.

Costume history books come in three general types. The first type covers a comprehensive history of fashion in a single volume, usually covering eras from prehistory to the twentieth century. These books are useful for a general overview of a period, but because they include such a large amount of material, they are not able to cover many specifics.

Books that specialize in one era is the second type. These can report on a period's many nuances, from differences in social class, economics, race, culture, gender, politics, religion, age, and many more. What it lacks in range of periods, it makes up for in detail.

The third type is books on patterning or construction. These describe building methods, both period construction and modern ways to adapt the garment. They may also have patterns, some taken from actual existing clothes. Janet Arnold's series *Patterns of Fashion* offers eighth scale drafts of actual garments along with extensive notations on the construction method. A designer can use this to accurately recreate a garment just as it was worn in the period, or they can use the material to adapt to modern needs.

Many varieties of art history books exist, but a costume designer will encounter three main types: Museum exhibits, a compilation of an artist's body of work, and a collection of work categorized by time period.

Books on specific collections or exhibits in museums can offer research into specific themes. From the history of punk to contemporary Muslim fashions, these resources can provide insight into the characteristics of a distinct style of art or subcultures.

Books that document an artist's complete works are useful for designers who need to familiarize themselves with a particular aesthetic approach, especially if they desire the costume design to emulate that artist. Artists like Gustav Klimt and Pablo Picasso have a recognizable look that can serve as inspiration for a designer's own aesthetic.

Art history books that document an era in time is helpful for the designer who needs an overview on a period in history. A book may explore many regions and showcase how artists interpreted their own world, which gives a designer context.

Costume and art history books can be costly to buy, but many are available through libraries. Unlike general searches on the Internet, sources in costume books are simple to verify, especially with the help of librarians who are trained to find information in databases. They may offer interlibrary loans and subscribe to academic peer-reviewed journals, significantly increasing materials. The library may have fewer resources than the Internet, but it makes up for it in reliable information.

With a collection of historical information from good sources, a designer will be able to translate the proper silhouette onto their characters. Good research is a designer's foundation, especially when authenticity is the appeal of the show.

For a Fantastical or Surreal Setting

Some shows are set in a world that has no historical precedent. Fantasies like *Alice in Wonderland* start in the real world, but the character Alice is soon transported to an enchanted forest populated with anxious rabbits, a smoking caterpillar, and a tired dormouse. The design team might want to set a show like Shakespeare's *The Tempest* on an alien terrain with moon monsters and spirits. A show might need an abstract aesthetic meant to take place in a world that does not resemble anything known in our physical world. In these cases, in-depth historical research can still be useful. In a setting based on the surreal or fantastical, a designer will need to build a world that is both consistent and believable. Developing a silhouette that is logical to the world is a place to start. One can look to past cultures and times to study the silhouettes and how they were used. Designers can combine these looks to make a new silhouette for their world. For example, the eighteenth-century French court dress was characterized by wide gowns that extended the hips far beyond what is naturally human—these were called panniers. The 1980s were known for large shoulder pads and big hair styles. Even if the average person didn't wear the most outlandish fashions that defined the decade, they represented an ideal. A designer can pick and choose interesting elements from both these periods. History can serve as a baseline to create new fashions and cohesive designs.

A designer should also observe other subjects for inspiration: favorite artists, musicians, nature, technology. A favorite painting may influence a color scheme for the show. A moving piece of music might evoke a particular energy or mood. A designer can create costumes that match that mood with their fabric and texture choices. A walk in the forest could bring out ideas for a costume's material and texture. Influences can be found anywhere. A designer should be creative, going beyond Internet search engines for a well-rounded design.

RESEARCH ON THE INTERNET: THE GOOD, THE BAD, AND THE UGLY

Books, museums, and libraries are marvelous resources, but the Internet age has brought a new wealth of information that would be foolish to ignore. But, with a digital space offering endless options, finding useful information can be challenging, especially when anyone can post anything to a large platform. It is both a designer's most significant advantage and disadvantage; access to information is both easy and instantly available. However, a designer might have to sort through scores of misinformation before finding a useful article or website. Research is also made complex because the information is not a binary of "good" and "bad"; it is a spectrum of "relevant," "trivial," "unimportant," "inspiring," and everything in between.

A common strategy for new designers is to open an Internet image search engine, type in a vague descriptor of the concept (i.e., "Italian Cinema") and save the first few results. It is an efficient strategy, but the process is inherently shallow. Internet search engines are not inherently the wrong place to begin research, but a designer must know how to find deep information and recognize good sources.

Research tactics can differ based on the goal. A search for a realistic historical drama will require different sources than a surreal or fantastical story, but useful information is required regardless of the setting. With limitless information available, knowing some red flags may cull the research pile.

The most basic red flag to look for on a website is bad formatting and spelling errors. If a blogger does not put in the effort to proofread or make the website legible, chances are they did not care to fact check the information. These websites should be ignored. Far better information can be found on any other site. Another flag is the lack of credited sources. A missing bibliography does not necessarily mean the material on the website is false, but if a reference isn't provided, the designer should cross-check the facts with a reputable source. Computer algorithms encourage a large number of clicks to generate ad revenue. Video creators and blog writers are incentivized to skip the fact-checking phase for the sake of posting content quickly. Educational and reputable non-profit organizations that favor quality over quantity are generally safer sources.

Some bloggers may also fall into the "Hollywood is the same as history" trap. Popular movies aren't designed to be historically accurate, even the ones that have a strong historical theme. Popular films and other media are meant to appeal to a contemporary aesthetic, and so they bend aspects of history to appear more pleasing to the modern eye. Otherwise, we'd have many more medieval based films where the characters would have a thick layer of dirt on their skin, as it was thought dirt kept illness out of their body (Herman, 2018). This is not a flaw in these films. They're not meant to be educational tools; they're meant to tell a compelling story to a mass audience.

The 1963 film *Cleopatra*—a stunning achievement in costume design history that won Oscars for its three designers Nino Novarese, Renié, and Irene Sharaff—takes many liberties with the Ptolemaic period in Egypt. Silk was used instead of linen due to linen's tendency to wrinkle. Garments were tailored in to show Elizabeth Taylor's figure. Women didn't have shaved heads as they would have had in that time.

The costume design is even more modernized in the 2012 action horror movie *Abraham Lincoln: Vampire Hunter*. The character Vadoma is dressed in tight trousers and sleeves tied onto a bodice, an ensemble that would be odd in the 1860s, but was typical in stores in the early 2010s. While both these styles are perfect for these big-budget films—the former showing off the spectacle of lavish costumes, the latter intended for campy popcorn fun—they are not meant for period research. Their value is in artistic inspiration and admiration for their work in the field.

A designer may be able to tell if a website is using non-historical references by looking at the images displayed—are they portraits or extant garments? Or are they from a film or a costume from a Renaissance festival? Some of these websites aren't deliberately trying to mislead. They may have some purpose other than research, like selling reproduction garments for cosplayers. It is up to the designer to use their best critical thinking when approaching websites.

Related to "Hollywood mistaken for history" trap is misattribution. Paintings or garments about a period in history may not be from that period. Modern artists may be able to convincingly paint in the style of a medieval work, which can fool a researcher into believing in its authenticity. As mentioned above, it is not necessarily malicious intentions by an artist (though it can be), just an act of mislabeling when others appropriate the art. The painting *The Accolade* by Edmund Leighton depicts a young queen bestowing knighthood upon a young man in chainmail and a tabard. The scene is vaguely medieval, and to those untrained in art history, it might be mistaken as an authentic medieval painting. But Edmund Leighton painted it in 1901, making it an interpretation of the period rather than a primary source. Like films, it can be used for artistic inspiration, but not historical research.

For websites that a designer can generally trust, one might look for web addresses that end in *edu*, *org*, or *ac* followed by the country's code (e.g., *website.ac.uk* for the United Kingdom or *website.ac.jp* for Japan). These originate from academic or research organizations and may be contacted if a designer has additional questions not available on the website.

"How Historically Accurate Do I Need to Be?"

The last section mentioned that Hollywood had no obligation to be historically accurate. It exists to tell a story that earns revenue, not to educate. If artistic liberties are both intended and encouraged, is extensive and precise historical research needed?

In any medium, there will always be practical concerns that prevent historical purity: A zipper may be inserted into a period dress if the actor needs to change quickly; the original style of textiles may no longer exist; obtaining historical materials could be illegal in the modern day, i.e., whalebones that were once used to make corset busks. On the artistic side, the director may want a hint of a historical period while still maintaining a fashionable appeal to audiences—television shows aimed at teenagers use this style.

The level of historical accuracy depends on the project. To figure out what is right for the designer's show, one must consider the intent and appeal. If a show is designed to portray characters emulating real life (i.e., realism), or if a show's purpose is an exaggeration of life (i.e., a farce or slapstick comedy), then the clothes can be embellished to reflect that mood.

Audiences have an expectation when they engage in certain types of media. Those that enjoy historical reenactments expect a precise level of accuracy. Period dramas are sometimes referred to as "costume dramas" because the audience comes in wanting to see spectacular gowns and stately suits or doublets. It is the costume equivalent of an action movie explosion; part of the fun of these shows is seeing how people dressed in the past. Going against those expectations may invite annoyance, anger, or bad reviews (a later chapter will discuss the merits of subverting audience expectations).

In shows where the appeal is less about accuracy and more about the fantastical, weird, or outlandish, there is more room to twist elements of the period. But that doesn't mean one can ignore history altogether. Having a strong foundation in a period informs a designer about possibilities. From there, a designer can take liberties while still maintaining a believable world. A strong knowledge of history can also inspire more stylistic ideas. In the 2012 movie *Mirror, Mirror* directed by Tarsem Singh Dhandwar, costume designer Eiko Ishioka takes heavy inspiration from sixteenth and seventeenth-century European dress, with touches of the eighteenth and nineteenth century. On that foundation, she added plenty of her own brilliant flare to bring all the elements together into a cohesive unit. Knowledge of fashion history gave her more tools to work with, adding layers to their work. The design of that movie would not have existed if the designer was unfamiliar with centuries of fashion.

Audience members and movie-goers are astute, and they aren't shy about writing stern posts on social media regarding egregious errors. They'll know if something feels "off" even if they don't have the background knowledge to express precisely what. It might come in the form of reviews resembling, "The show looked like a beauty vlogger on YouTube, not a period drama," or "When did Marie Antoinette start shopping at the mall?" These are an audience's way of saying a show or film felt too modern for the style they expected. No formula exists that will achieve perfect results every time. It is a lifelong experiment of trial-and-error.

EXAMPLE: RESEARCHING A CONCEPTUAL DESIGN

This section will explore a theoretical designer's research process using the *Much Ado About Nothing* example from the preceding chapter. The following is just one of the many possibilities, but it should help to guide a curious designer who does not know where to start.

Hypothetical Concept: *Much Ado About Nothing*, but with a Teen Vampire Aesthetic of the Mid-2000s Mixed with the Rococo Era of Art

Fantasy has a strong foundation in history. Neither of these styles is directly related; therefore, they might look for a common thread between them while researching. In the end, the design will need to be cohesive.

The first research task is to search "Rococo." If the designer had no prior knowledge of the term, a sufficient place to begin would be Wikipedia. Wikipedia gives enough of an overview for a designer to familiarize themselves with the basic concepts and terminology, giving them enough of a foundation to search other places effectively.

According to Wikipedia,

> Rococo ... less commonly rococo, or "Late Baroque," is an exceptionally decorative and theatrical style of decoration which combines asymmetry, scrolling curves, gilding, white and pastel colors, sculpted molding, and trompe l'oeil frescoes to create the illusions of surprise, motion, and drama. It first appeared in France and Italy in the 1730s and spread to Central Europe in the 1750s and 1760s. It is often described as the final expression of the Baroque movement.

Wikipedia gives a clue that the style is going to need a lot of detail, probably in the form of trims or fabric that is patterned or embroidered. Rococo originated in the middle of the eighteenth century, which could be used as a foundation for developing this world's silhouette.

Wikipedia's article links to the Victoria and Albert Museum's website, a museum of art and design in London, England. (The Rococo page can be found at www.vam.ac.uk/collections/rococo) The web page gives a summary of the style, then links to pictures of artifacts from the museum's collection. Familiar patterns start to emerge in the textures and patterns. Gold and ivory color dominate the photographs with extravagant motifs inspired by asymmetrical natural shapes: vines, flowers, seashells, and mosses.

A common type of gown was the robe à la Francaise, also known as the sack-back gown, so called because of the waterfall of fabric that spilled from the back of the bodice. Many of the court gowns had dense, floral patterns in silk brocade fabric. Golds, blues, and creams are frequently used colors, along with orange and red fringe for the trim. The dresses are flamboyant yet striking. The silhouette changes through the decades, but the most extravagant dresses meant for formal events have wide panniers that can span up to five feet. This extreme silhouette might be suited for the party scene in *Much*

Ado. The exaggerated proportions lend themselves to the comedy in the scene, offering opportunities for farcical shenanigans in the blocking. For now, the designer could make note of it.

The designer next looks at books that specialize in eighteenth-century fashion. *18th Century Fashion in Detail* by Susanna North shows not only the silhouette, but has enlarged photographs of the buttons, pockets, embroidery, and pleats. The designer could place bookmarks at specific details that strike them as being relevant to particular characters. Maybe one distinct trim looks fitting for Hero's party gown or a style of breeches encompasses a perfect "romantic lead" for Claudio. They go through all the characters and ponder how they might fit in with this style.

Now that the designer has thoroughly researched the eighteenth-century silhouette and the Rococo style, they move on to studying the teen vampire romance aesthetic from the mid-2000s. They first investigate how the vampire genre evolved. They look into old Slavic myths, Bram Stoker's *Dracula*, the Universal Studio Monsters, Anne Rice's *Lestat* novels, and finally, to the YA supernatural trend popularized by Stephanie Meyer's novel *Twilight*. They research films and art in history and find out how the aesthetics of vampires changed throughout history. The designer may make a note to talk with the director about possibly combining elements of past versions of vampire lore for more variety.

The designer also might worry the references could feel dated. There's a fine line between "retro," "vintage," "classic," and "unfashionable." They might make a note to ask about the intention behind the concept. Is it to appeal to nostalgia? Or is it to pay homage to a popular aesthetic of a certain period?

The designer could also watch the movies that were part of the cultural movement and note not only the styles and colors of clothing but also the color grade of the film itself. The research on Rococo revealed the standard colors to be white, pastels, and golds. In the modern movies on vampires, the colors lean toward a seafoam green, blues, oranges, and reds.

After the designer is confident in my research, they gather up my notes and write down questions for the director and the rest of the team. The next step is another discussion followed by the first design sketches.

SUMMARY

- Organization and paperwork at the beginning of the design process will help the production process move more smoothly.
- Costume plots track the number of costumes in a show. It also maps the characters' changes by scene.
- The production schedule notes important events like production meetings, photo calls, and the tech schedule.
- The concept of the show is a collaborative effort among a whole team, including the costume, set, lighting, sound, and projection designer along with directors, stage managers, and choreographers.
- To research historical settings, primary sources are the most accurate information followed by secondary and tertiary sources. The Internet has compiled more readily accessible information than ever before, but there are tricks to know how to avoid faulty or inaccurate data.

3

DEVELOPMENT OF THE DESIGN, SKETCHING, AND PAINTING A RENDERING

DESIGN DEVELOPMENT

After the first meeting, a designer will gather their historical and conceptual research, consider the notes from the director, and use that information to create the first costume sketches. Before digging into the artistic side of design, the following sections detail points a designer should keep in mind as their character design develops.

Appeal

When creating the costume design, there are four components to consider in the process:

What the script and story need.
What the audience needs.
What the designer needs.
What the team needs.

Each of these are linked together in many ways, but individually, they don't always need equal weight—that depends on the show. Balancing each gives different effects.

One effective strategy is to put the needs of the story first. To do this means that the designer makes choices that highlight themes, enhances character, and allows the audience to focus on dialogue.

An effective costume design that emphasizes story will make the characters feel real to the world in which they live, allowing the audience to immerse themselves.

The reaction of the audience ties in with serving the story, though they are a separate entity to consider. Immersion in the story can be a desirable outcome, but a costume designer can consider the possibility of breaking immersion if it suits the themes the director and the design team want to convey. This could mean surprising the crowd with shocking imagery to draw attention to one specific thing. Or, a visual gag can add laughter to an otherwise dry moment.

Designers can put emphasis on their own artistic desires. Doing this can evoke a certain passion and make a project more personal. When a designer feels ownership of their work, it creates a project that is not only enjoyable to work on, but also produces a product that feels unique. However, going too far with personal style might make a design that emphasizes personal taste over everything else, which could distract from the story. Context matters; when in doubt, consider what the story needs.

Personal artistic desires tie into the needs of the team. As discussed before, collaboration between colleagues creates the store, but each team member's individuality can bring new ideas. Audiences can perceive when artists have excitement for their work. Complete subservience to others' opinions will lack a personal passion integral to an artist's work, which could lead to a bland design.

A designer may also put aside any of the four components listed above, which is a valid choice to make. For instance, some shows with challenging messages may want to provoke the audience intentionally. Angering the patrons may be the whole point of the play, while in other shows, angering the audience may not fare well for ticket sales. Different kinds of theater, film, and television serve different purposes and have different intents. A commercial theater designed to appeal to a mass audience may want the designers to make safer choices. However, some theaters exist to make artistic statements and thus may desire something shocking enough to spark conversations. If a costume designer is unsure about a specific audience's appeal, a discussion with the director or the marketing team can aid with the decision.

Culture, Symbols, and Other Representative Imagery

A symbol is something that represents something else, e.g., a red heart represents love and friendship or flags that represent countries. How people interpret those images depends on the culture, region, or individual.

How much should a costume designer rely on symbolic imagery? Ultimately, design is about communication. The designer can determine just how much is necessary to convey their intended meaning.

There are different levels to audience understanding. An audience will probably not think, "The blue represents her sadness." Their knowledge will come in the form of emotions rather than direct thoughts. A scene with cold light, blue colors, and slow, somber music may make a western audience associate the moment with sadness because these are cues that their culture has assigned a melancholy meaning. With a good design, an audience may be able to feel these emotions without needing words or dialogue to tell them. The best way to bring out that sentiment is to understand how culture and imagery affects human emotion and how people react to visuals based on their own personal experiences and biases.

One job of the designer is to find the right balance when using cultural significant images and symbols. Depending on the play and the audience, a designer can choose to be blunt with their meaning or be subtle. For example, in a serious drama, dressing a greedy character in a green suit with dollar signs on it might put off an audience rather than engage them. The audience that loves serious dramas will likely understand and internalize subtlety. Subtler character design is needed to accurately portray a greedy character that has depth. To contrast, shows targeted at children will usually involve easily recognized and understood imagery. The man with the dollar-sign suit would fit perfectly in a young children's play.

Some symbols carry the same meaning across the world, but many are culturally specific. One way to learn how an audience understands symbols is to pay attention to the playwrights from those regions and note how they use imagery to convey emotion.

Shakespeare's language shows the use of imagery and its connection with a person's emotional reaction. If a designer goes back to the text analysis, they can find symbols and imagery within the text that will evoke ideas for rendering. In this passage from *Much Ado About Nothing*, Beatrice confesses her love for Benedick.

BEATRICE:
What fire is in mine ears? Can this be true?
Stand I condemn'd for pride and scorn so much?
Contempt, farewell! and maiden pride, adieu!
No glory lives behind the back of such.
And, Benedick, love on; I will requite thee,
Taming my wild heart to thy loving hand:
If thou dost love, my kindness shall incite thee
To bind our loves up in a holy band;
For others say thou dost deserve, and I
Believe it better than reportingly.

The words in this passage have stated emotions that can be turned into visual imagery for the costume rendering. "Fire" here is used in the same way modern society uses "my ears are burning"—as in, the person knows someone else is gossiping about them. Also, Beatrice describes being in love as "taming" a "wild" heart, drawing a connection to animals and nature. She also uses "bind" to refer to matrimony, another motif that is familiar in the modern-day. All of these words can be used to create a design that communicates these feelings—one can imagine a costume that resembles a "binding" to a character that is "wildfire" personified.

A designer can experiment with imagery by sketching out ideas. For example, let's explore an object that evokes specific emotions—a "cage." Cages are synonymous with the lack of freedom, loneliness, cold, and punishment. An artist can make an audience think of cages by just painting vertical lines spaced close together in a cool color. Costume designers can use that same technique in clothing. If characters are dressed in constricting clothes with style lines that mirror bars, an audience will imprint similar feelings that are associated with a cage.

Much of this interpretation of imagery, however, depends on the context. Red is a color that, in western cultures, can mean both passion or death, depending on the situation. The color red placed in a sultry setting—a date night, a bordello with warm, intimate lighting—will feel passionate. The color red painted in a house of horror with severed body parts and bathtubs of blood will feel terrifying.

In western art, an angel is often portrayed in white robes with big white wings and bathed in white light. This is because, in this context, western society has assigned white to mean "pure" and "good." If the angel were changed to wear red—the color associated with hell, the angel's opposite—it would change how an audience reads the character. They might see the angel as being rebellious or indulgent in wicked activities.

Designers can also combine symbols to create something new. Using the cage imagery, imagine if the show's aesthetic wanted a cage but not the cage's negative associations. What if the cage needed to be framed positively? Mix and matching ideas have different effects. A designer could perhaps design a bodice with vertical lines that indicate a cage but color the "bars" in warm, inviting tones.

A trial-and-error approach to design is not uncommon. Exploring through sketches and paintings can help find the proper balance for each character.

Shorthand

Shorthand is imagery that draws on cultural symbols an audience already knows. Its purpose is to communicate information quickly.

A character dressed in a white button-down shirt, a pocket protector, and glasses taped together at the bridge will immediately be known to an audience as a "nerd" without that character having to say or do anything. This is shorthand. While this design represents a caricature rather than an attempt to emulate a real person, it gets the idea communicated to the audience swiftly. While this tool may not be desired for plays with emotional or intellectual depth, large musicals meant for mainstream entertainment will rely on shorthand. These shows can have dozens of characters in small parts (named in the script by their role, like "an ice-cream seller," "a beatnik," "a soldier," etc.) that may get one line. It is up to the costumes and the actor to communicate the character.

Shorthand is related to **tropes** (a storytelling device that is familiar to an audience) and clichés (something that is so overused that it becomes tired), but it is not always something to avoid. The tricky thing about art is that there are never absolutes. Reasons exist that justify any decision. Experimentation breeds experience, which will lead to better designs. Understand the world and what it means to people, and that will help translate the script into a costume design.

SKETCHING IDEAS

Sketching is a way to brainstorm different options before committing to a particular look. With a series of quick drawings, a designer can experiment with varying shapes and lines to see what best suits the character and style. Sketches also give the director a sense of what approach the designer intends for the costumes. Added color swatches to the sketch will also help communicate the design's mood and energy.

After another round of discussions, the director will give notes on the sketches. The designer then makes revisions to their drawings before presenting them again. The process continues until the team settles on a look everyone is happy with. When the director approves the costume designer's ideas, a designer will precede to paint full-color **costume renderings** to represent the final look.

Renderings are a promise to the director and the other team members to coordinate with the set, lighting, and sound. These elements must complement each other. To break the promise is to break the other designers' work as well. When a designer chooses shapes, colors, and textures, the others can use that information to integrate their own work. For example, if a designer chooses a fitted green dress with wide, sweeping skirts, a lighting designer uses cool lights to enhance the color. The set designer could plan for the size of the skirt and design staircases and doorways to accommodate the fullness. If there is a choreographer, they can design a dance that uses the flow of the fabric. If the costume design changes, it could affect the other team members' work in significant ways.

The first ideas need not be the only ideas. They are a designer's first draft, rough ideas laid out on paper. Figure 3.1 shows different drafts as the designer tests different styles. From the drawings, a designer can evaluate the effectiveness of the concept as applied to each character. They can also refer to the research for historical and character authenticity. From there, a second, third, or fourth draft is sketched depending on the complexity of the show, each with more detail than the last. Designers can alter sketches as many times as needed. During the development of a costume, a designer may change only

Figure 3.1 Costume designers test out various ideas using quick sketches.

small details or the entire costume could need revised. These changes are crucial to building a well-developed design. A costume designer should be open to new information, whether that is from director notes, from research, or from outside inspirations.

Sketching all the characters allows the designer to see a broader view of the work. Consideration should be given to how all the characters fit together. Keeping the big picture in mind creates a cohesive design overall. If too much focus is spent on the individual rather than the whole, the costumes might feel disjointed.

SKETCHING STRATEGIES

Strong costume sketches come from practice. For a beginner, tracing images with pencils can be a good way to start developing a sense of the human body. From there, a designer can move beyond tracing to a quick drawing technique called a **croquis**. These fast drawings encourage the designer to look at a person's general proportion and movement. Once they have a good grasp on the ways a body can be posed and how a body is shaped, a designer can start refining their skills with longer drawing sessions. Using live models is a good way to learn drawing from life, but any reference image that encourages the designer to practice will help. This knowledge is useful in creating drawings that portray a lively character.

For the drawing of clothing, a designer can first start to practice sketching different kinds of fabric draped over objects. This will help train the eye to recognize the various ways fabric can fold and hang. Further fabric studies can be done by observing clothing in everyday life. A designer can look at how clothing creases as a person sits or pulls when a person bends.

With sketching costumes, a good pose is a great tool to communicate the qualities of a character to the director and the team. It shows not only what the costume might look like, but it conveys a view of who the character could become.

FUNDAMENTALS OF DESIGN

The fundamentals of design are the foundation of visual art, made up of many elements. Shape, line, texture, color, scale, balance, unity, and emphasis/focus are the primary tools used to build the structure of the work, called a **composition**.

These foundational elements are also used in costumes where a designer that uses these elements effectively can create a striking image on stage.

Line

In geometry, lines are a two-dimensional object created by connecting two points. Our eyes naturally follow the lines' direction, giving it a natural sense of movement. An artist can alter the quality of a line to evoke certain moods or to draw attention to specific sections of the drawing. A line's weight—that is, its thickness or thinness—changes the artwork's perceived mass. Thin lines feel light and airy, while thick lines give the drawing a heaviness as seen in Figure 3.2. Messy lines feel chaotic and energetic, while orderly, uniform lines give the impression of a strict structure.

Physical lines don't have to be drawn for one to be present. Implied lines, also known as psychic lines, exist along paths created

Figure 3.2 Line weight, thickness, and quality affect the composition of a work.

Figure 3.3 The eyeline of a group of actors is an example of leading an audience using an invisible line.

by pointing objects. Eye lines—in which a person instinctually looks where other people are watching—are a type of psychic line. Directors use this technique when blocking a scene. When the actors collectively look at the same thing, the audience will look there, too, as shown in Figure 3.3. A series of buttons or a pattern of dots on fabric can create a psychic line.

For a costume designer, the line of a garment is an essential asset and is evident in the language of fashion. An A-line skirt resembles a similar image as the titular letter "A." Crisp and heavy fabrics like taffeta create sharp lines when pleated. Striped fabric can be arranged to direct the eye toward the face.

Shape and Form

When a line joins to form an enclosure, a shape is created. Shapes put together in specific ways can represent people, objects, or forms. Figure 3.4 contains shapes that suggest a person. When a shape is given volume and mass, it becomes a three-dimensional form. Everything a designer creates, including the silhouette of a garment, is built with shapes: circular, boxy, straight, curvilinear, and so on. The buttons, trim, accessories, fabric print, and hair are all configurations of form that have been combined to create a design.

A designer can play with scale, proportion, and variety of their shapes. Wide sleeves and a large skirt can make a waist seem narrow. Outfits can combine colors and mix patterns to create compelling visual textures. A costume designer can even exaggerate the natural scale of the body.

Figure 3.4 Shapes clustered together can suggest the idea of objects and people.

Texture

Texture describes the property of a surface, relating closely to the sense of touch. Something textural can be gritty, soft, rough, slimy, wet, mushy, gummy, smooth, and an infinite array of others. A sleek satin silk differs significantly from a prickly fur, which in turn differs from the feel of gravel and rock. But all can be combined to create a dynamic composition.

Fabrics come in many textures. Wool can be itchy while linen is airy and cool. Silk is smooth and soft against the skin. Designers can also manipulate fabrics to add more texture. Smocking, embroidery, crystals, and trim can add energy and life to a garment.

In a costume rendering, a designer can simulate textures with painting techniques. Line weight, stroke quality, highlights, and shadows can create convincing paintings that evoke many textures, including fur or velvet. A designer can also apply dimensional objects to their renderings for an extra sense of touch.

Harmony

A composition must look like all the elements belong together. For costumes, this applies to both the big picture and within a single garment. In the big picture, all the garments together on stage must work as a cohesive unit. Even if characters in a story have different personalities, they must still look like they come from the same world. Harmony, however, doesn't necessarily mean everything is the same. A series of beige-colored shapes might have unity, but it may not have much visual interest. There is unity in variety as long as each element carries components of each other.

Within a costume, harmony is created by mirroring colors, lines, and textures on all parts of an outfit, including the jewelry, hats, and shoes. Hats and jewelry can bring a costume together, completing it. All the elements should make sense together.

Emphasis/Focus

Emphasis happens when one thing contrasts with the others, causing it to stand out among them. When an artist needs to accentuate something in a composition, they can emphasize it with a variety

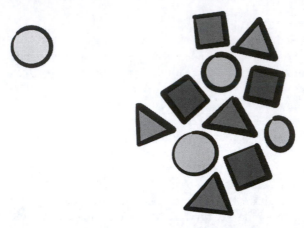

Figure 3.5 Emphasis is created when a lone object is set apart from a group.

of methods. Isolation is one tactic as demonstrated in Figure 3.5. If a chaotic pattern has a blank area, that spot will draw attention. One object that is different from all other objects also pulls focus. A circle, for instance, will stand out in a collection of triangles. One green stripe in a collection of red stripes will become the focal point of that object.

In addition, one can draw focus using lines. People's eyes follow lines, and if many point to a single spot, then that section will have an audience's attention. Figure 3.6 shows lines that lead the eye to a circle in the center. It is why arrows work so effectively to get people to look at a certain point. The placement of an object will change emphasis too, with the center being a strong area for focus.

Balance

Balance is how a composition is "weighted." If an artist places every object in a painting on one side of the canvas, and nothing on the other, the result will feel uneven. A balanced canvas can feel natural, calm, and satisfying. However, too much balance and too much symmetry can be tedious. Art is meant to make people feel things, so an

Figure 3.6 Objects pointing to a single spot will draw the eye of a viewer.

uneasiness in the imbalance may be a desirable outcome. How does one tell the difference between ineffective imbalance and effective imbalance?

There is a balance in asymmetry if one thinks of a canvas as a scale. Too much on one side—whether that be top, bottom, left, or right—will tip those scales too far. The other side needs a counterweight. Figure 3.7 uses the isolation technique to create emphasis, but in doing so it has created an imbalanced image with all the heaviness biased toward the right.

Costumes can be approached similarly to a canvas. The body has a left and right, up and down. A small, tightly fitted bodice can contrast a large, voluminous skirt—it would be asymmetrical in the up-and-down, but symmetrical in its left and right. Trim and fabric patterns can lend a feeling of balance or imbalance. A plaid shirt has a regular repeating pattern all over. But what if one sleeve was plaid while the other was polka dot? Depending on the context, this could be a contrived design (if the character was a strait-laced businessman), or it could be perfect in its asymmetry (if the character was someone like the Mad Hatter from Lewis Carroll's *Alice in Wonderland*). The context of the story and concept is key to determining the proper balance.

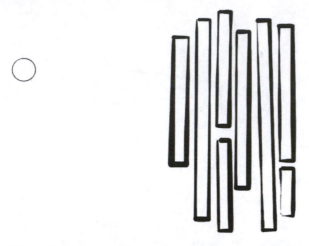

Figure 3.7 A heavy amount of activity on one side of the composition can make the work feel imbalanced.

COLOR THEORY

While the previously mentioned elements of design give a costume shape, color elevates a costume, giving it a sense of life. *The Wizard of Oz*, a film produced by Metro-Goldwyn-Mayer, used color to bring a sense of awe to a story where such a dramatic and brilliant scene was not expected. Color transforms the way people tell stories. It is not a "thing" that can be touched or felt like fabric or paper; it is a small segment of light, the key to vision.

People have used color in both the practical sense and the artistic sense. Color dictates the flow of traffic with stop signs and traffic lights. A sport uses color so the players and the crowd can identify the people that play for their team. It has been used in idioms to impart sensibilities, such as with the phrases, "feeling blue" or "green with envy."

Artists throughout history have found ways to manipulate light and color to trigger emotions and inspire the imagination. Color is a crucial tool, one that can make a costume look sublime if cleverly used. A costume designer must understand how color works before it can be employed effectively.

What Color Is Made of and Why It Matters for a Costume Designer

Color is made of light, which means light affects the color of a costume. Previous chapters talked about collaboration with the team, but that partnership goes beyond the discussion of ideas. Knowledge of the other designers' color choices can enhance the costume design because color changes depending on the context in which it is used. This section talks about light and why a costumer should consider it as they design.

Light is a spectrum made up of wavelengths. On the infrared end of this spectrum, those waves are close together. On the ultraviolet end, the waves are spaced far apart. This is called **frequency**. Most of these wavelengths are invisible to the human eye: gamma rays, x-rays, radio waves, microwaves. Humans can see only a narrow slice of this spectrum, and that is where the colors we perceive come from. Not all people see color the same way. A typical human eye has three color-sensitive cones—blue, green, and red. Some eyes only have two of those cones fully activated, which means people with reduced sensitivity to specific colors see a narrower piece of the visible light spectrum.

Isaac Newton first discovered that light was made of color when he placed a prism in a sunbeam, and it split into a rainbow on the wall. He identified seven colors in that rainbow—red, orange, yellow, green, blue, indigo, and violet—to mirror the seven music notes on the diatonic scale. Newton arranged these colors into a circle forming the first color wheel (Brody 2015).

Scientists discovered that objects absorb light and reflect specific wavelengths into our eyes. That is, an object that appears yellow is absorbing all visible light except yellow. When an object is pure black, we are seeing an absence of light; no photons are being reflected. When we see white, all color wavelengths are reaching our eye.

When an artist mixes paints, they are changing how waves of light interact with objects. With a basic understanding, a designer can learn to manipulate and blend any color of their choosing with precision.

There are two types of color wheel that a designer will need to know—the color wheel of light and the color wheel of pigment.

The Color Wheel of Pigment

Color wheels start with the three **primaries**. The primaries are foundational colors that are used to create all other hues. No color can be mixed to create a primary. In the color wheel of pigment, the primary colors are red, yellow, and blue (oftentimes shortened to **RYB**).

When two primary colors are mixed, they create **secondary colors**. Red blended with yellow produces orange. Yellow and blue make green. Blue and red form violet. These six colors—red, orange, yellow, green, blue, and violet—make a basic six-color wheel. A color wheel, however, can go infinitely deep. The **tertiary colors** are created by mixing a primary color and a secondary color: Red and orange make red-orange; orange and yellow make yellow-orange; yellow and green make yellow-green; green and blue make blue-green; blue and violet make blue-violet. The primaries, secondaries, and tertiaries make a twelve-color wheel.

A common question arises when regarding color mixing: If two primary colors make a secondary color, and one primary and one secondary makes a tertiary color, what happens when two secondary colors are mixed? The color wheel itself can answer many of these kinds of questions. Orange is a mixture of red and yellow. Green is a mixture of yellow and blue. The components that make up two secondary colors include all three primary colors. Mixing two secondaries would be the same as mixing three primaries. The result is a muddy grey-brown. In theory, mixing all primaries should produce black, but pigments are not chemically perfect enough to reflect the genuine primaries. Blues, reds, and yellows can vary between companies.

Mixing paints takes practice. Results can vary even if the pigments are carefully measured. Red blended with yellow can produce a different kind of orange than yellow blended in with red. A pigment's materials can also favor one color over another. A designer should experiment with different brands and different tones of reds, yellows, and blues to see what combination produces the most desirable results.

When an artist mixes two pigments, it is called **subtractive mixing**. It is counterintuitive to think adding colors together is subtracting, but the term comes from how the artist affects the light.

Mixing pigments blocks wavelengths from reaching the eye—if a person wants to see blue, they must subtract the green and red wavelengths. Because black means no color enters the eye, an artist must subtract all waves to achieve the desired result.

There is a second subtractive color model that is worth noting: **CMYK**, which stands for the primary colors cyan, magenta, yellow, and black. The secondary colors for the CMYK model are red, green, and blue. This color wheel is used in color printing. Costume designers will need CMYK if their renderings are digital. In software editing programs like Adobe Photoshop, a designer can work in CMYK mode if the intent is to print the renderings or sketches. The other mode that software programs offer is called **RGB**, which is best used for artwork that will be displayed on monitors and the web. The next section will detail more on the RGB color model.

The Color Wheel of Light

Light has different properties than pigment. When light is mixed together, it is called **additive mixing**, because the artist is adding wavelengths instead of taking them away as with paints. When all colors are combined, the result is pure white light.

The three primaries of light are red, green, and blue (shortened to RGB), which correspond to the cones in the human eye. For the secondary colors, green and red make yellow; red and blue make magenta, and green and blue make cyan. The secondary colors of RGB are the same colors that make up the primaries of the CMYK color model.

A costume designer's predominant use of the RGB model is in collaboration with the lighting designer. Lighting changes the color of the costume. If a lighting designer plans to use a lot of blue light in a scene, a costume designer may want to avoid using red unless a dull, grey look is desired. Poor collaboration between lighting and costumes could mean a color palette that looks grey and muddy.

The costume designer will also need to know the RGB model if they plan on their renderings being displayed on the web or on computer-based platforms. Monitors and televisions work using electron beams that hit red, green, and blue phosphors. Designing in RGB mode will help the computer display the truest sense of the color. If a rendering is drawn in CMYK and then converted, the colors may distort when translated.

Color Relationships

The order of the colors on the wheel is intentional. They're in a specific order based on relationships. Secondary colors are between their parent colors, and tertiary colors are between their parent and grandparent. Beyond parentage, the color wheel reveals thousands of other relationships. This section will discuss a few of the most common.

The color wheel can be split into warm and cool **temperatures**. The warm colors—red, orange, and yellow—are associated with heat, the sun, and passion. Green, blue, and violet make up the cool colors and are correlated with winter, water, forests, and relaxation. Each of these color groups is **analogous**, which means they are next to each other on the wheel. Color schemes that use analogous hues have the least amount of **contrast**.

Contrast is a comparison between two colors. Colors that are different from each other have high contrast, while similar colors have low contrast. In Figure 3.8, the boxes on the left are greyed versions of analogous colors. Because they don't have much contrast,

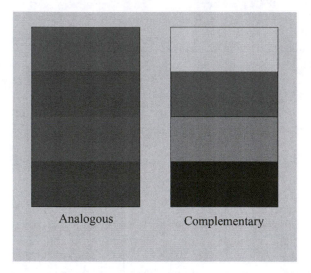

Analogous   Complementary

Figure 3.8 A comparison of analogous and complementary in grayscale.

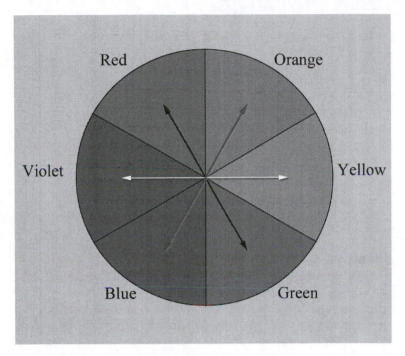

Figure 3.9 Complementary colors on a six-color wheel.

it is more difficult to distinguish between the two. The boxes on the right are greyed images of opposing colors. They have a high contrast, and thus are easier to tell apart.

Colors that have the highest amount of contrast are called **complementary colors**. Complementary colors are on the opposite side of the wheel, pictured in Figure 3.9. The complements on a six-color wheel are orange and blue, yellow and violet, and green and red. When an artist mixes complementary colors, they cancel each other out because all three primaries combined. Orange is a combination of yellow and red—when blended with blue, it mixes all the colors in the visible light spectrum.

Analogous and complementary color schemes serve different purposes for a costume designer. Analogous colors blend in with each other, making it harder for objects to stand out as an individual thing. Nothing projects or is unequal to anything else. A white gown in a white winter scene will make a character appear as if they "belong" in their world, as if they are one with it. Analogous colors also diffuse focus.

Complementary colors blend objects together. A character wearing a gown complementary in color to the surroundings will appear detached, independent from a world where they don't belong. Complementary colors draw focus. An audience will notice a yellow gown in a violet world because it is different from its surroundings.

The Neutrals

Three colors have yet to be addressed: Black, white, and gray. These colors are not represented on the standard color wheel. Black, white, and gray are **achromatic**, which means those colors have no **hue**. When a color is mixed, the result is another color, but when an *achromatic* color is mixed, the result is a lighter or darker version of that color.

Achromatic colors affect a hue's **value** and **saturation**. *Value* is a color's lightness or darkness, usually created by adding white or black. When white is added to a hue, it's called a **tint**: Pink is a tint of red. When black is added to a hue, it's called a **shade**: Crimson is a shade of red.

Saturation describes a color's neutrality, also called its grayness. Saturation is a spectrum—on one end, a color can be so desaturated that it becomes full achromatic gray. On the other end, the pure color is considered uncontaminated by gray. Fully saturated hues are striking and brilliant. Used in excess hues can portray a fantasy world. It works for children's shows or bright musicals. Desaturated hues lend themselves better to moody or somber stories. Dark and gritty shows that want to market themselves as being more adult often go for a desaturated color palette.

To desaturate a color with paints, an artist can add gray, but this can be difficult because a manufacturer's grays can be imperfect. Some are bluer or redder than others, adding impurities to the color mixture where color was not intended. Another way to desaturate a color is to add its complement. The more red that is introduced to a green, the more gray it will look.

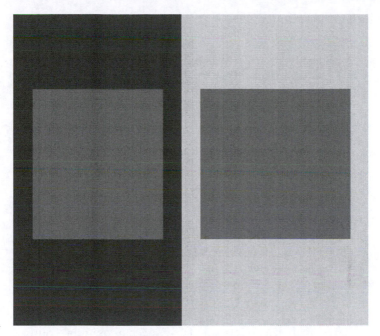

Figure 3.10 Viewers may perceive these gray boxes differently due to the contrasting backgrounds.

Adding black, white, or gray isn't the only way to change a color's value and saturation. Color is highly context-dependent. The human brain will process a hue differently based on what is around it.

In Figure 3.10, the square on the left is made to look brighter because of the dark background. The square on the right is made to look darker because of the white background. Artists have used this to create illusions.

In the same way the square's colors are altered based on the background, a set design can do the same thing to the color of the costumes. A buttery yellow dress will glow against a wine-colored background. But that same dress will appear not as bright if the set is a cream or alabaster color. It works within the costume, too. If a script has a necklace or amulet that the designer wants the audience to notice, it should have a color that contrasts the outfit. An audience will see a glittering red ruby on top of a dark forest green gown.

Color Combination

With millions of colors to choose from and a near-infinite amount of combinations, how does a designer choose which colors "go" together? A designer can first explore different **color schemes** to see which one resonates best with the intended design.

Monochromatic: "Chromatic" means "color" and "mono" means "one," so a monochromatic color scheme is made up of the same color in different values and saturations. This is useful when the designer wants to emphasize a dominant hue. A scene that is composed of tints and shades of red could evoke an excessive feeling of blood or a warning of danger. If the color scheme is all green, it could feel "sick." A monochromatic scene is good when nothing should stand out as an individual thing, and that all objects and people are part of the same elements. It is a visually cohesive scheme.

Analogous: Analogous color schemes use hues that are next to each other on the color wheel. "Warm" and "cool" are analogous variants, as mentioned above, but different combinations can be used depending on the desired amount of contrast. Yellow, green, and blue are analogous colors, but since yellow is warm, it'll contrast more than the green and blue. This color scheme is balanced and relaxed.

Complementary: This color scheme has the highest contrast. People and objects stand out as individual components in a complementary color scheme, as opposed to the monochromatic, where the elements blend. A complementary design can feel more energetic or chaotic and less harmonious.

Split-Complementary: This color scheme is similar to complementary, but it uses colors adjacent to the color's complement instead of the direct complement. Instead of using blue/orange as per the complementary color scheme, it would use blue, yellow-orange, and orange-red. It's not as turbulent as a complementary scheme, but it maintains a similar drama.

Triad: A triad scheme uses three colors that are evenly spaced on the wheel like blue, yellow-green, orange-red. Triad color schemes are vibrant. Though hard to balance, it is lively and expressive when used successfully.

These are five standard color schemes, but there are many more to explore. Each carries a different potential for particular characters and moods.

How to Determine Which Color Scheme Is Right for Your Design

Color has a symbolic meaning. Some of this meaning is universal—black evokes night and darkness while water is connected with the color blue—but some associations are culturally specific. Depending on the country, white can mean either purity or death. Red can mean either aggression or spirituality. One way to understand how color affects people is to observe how they are traditionally used in art, ritual, and in day-to-day life.

Brides in western culture traditionally wear white. Today, in western countries, it symbolizes virtue and spiritual cleanliness. How might some people react if the bride was dressed in red and black instead? A designer might think about what those colors mean and why people could have those kinds of responses. Merchandise marketed for Valentine's Day uses pink, reds, and whites. Red is commonly linked with heat, which in turn is affiliated with passion. Pink and whites are softer colors that symbolize a playful kind of love. With this in mind, consider a play with a romantic scene. How would a color scheme with arsenic green and brownish yellow-colored costumes affect the emotions of the scene? When might such a color scheme work, and when might it be less effective?

Figuring out how color affects emotions takes practice and experimentation. The answer is a lifelong journey of learning, observation, and experimentation with color and how it influences a person's feelings. Using the color scheme from a favorite painting that evokes the desired emotion can be a useful method in choosing colors for the costume design.

Along with the symbolic, color can serve a practical purpose. Graphic design on the internet is an excellent example of how people use color to guide a person's actions. As stated in the previous section, contrasting colors draw the eye, a technique utilized often in graphic design. On the Internet, links that read "Buy now!" are usually brightly colored on a neutral background while the "unsubscribe" or "close account" buttons are hidden behind dull links with a low contrast. Costume designers can use this technique, too, to draw the eye of the audience. Shiny bracelets that contrast a blouse can draw the eye to the hand. Vivid makeup paired with a neutral dress will draw the eye to the face.

Color can also be used to draw connections between characters. In a play like Shakespeare's *Romeo and Juliet*, the two families fighting each other is a significant part of the story. Color can define to which family the characters are loyal. Those allied with the Montagues can encompass one color scheme, while those allied with the Capulets can be another. Both family colors together on stage can be either complementary, analogous, or any other color combination. An argument can be made for any choice, but no matter what a designer chooses, the result will communicate different ideas.

As the designer determines the color scheme of any show, all the sketches of all the characters should be spread out so that connections and alliances can be noted—which characters need corresponding colors, and which need contrasting colors. This helps a designer develop a scheme that works well with the set and lighting design.

MOVING FROM SKETCHES TO COSTUME RENDERINGS

When a designer and the director is satisfied with the silhouette and the color scheme, the process of painting costume renderings can begin. During this phase, a designer will acquire fabric swatches that fit their color scheme and match the texture they desire. Details on fabric will be discussed in a later chapter.

AN ARTIST'S MEDIUM

A designer can choose any medium to paint their renderings. The decision will come down to the method that will best show the designer's artistic vision. Designers can explore different rendering tools to see which one complements their style best. Once they master that skill, they can build enough speed to produce dozens of renderings in a short amount of time. Practice helps build that speed.

PHYSICAL MEDIA

Watercolors

Watercolor is a type of paint that is—as the name implies—water-soluble. It is most commonly available in two types: pan and tube. Pan watercolor comes in dried cakes of pigment in a palette and is activated by water. Tube watercolor has a binder in it that gives it the consistency of toothpaste.

Water also controls the intensity of the paints. The less water used, the purer the color; more water changes the color's value. Watercolors are best painted with the dark hues first, and letting the white of the paper act as the highlight. When painted on wet paper, watercolor can achieve an elegant, feathery look. If a tube or cake has dried, water can reactivate it.

When used in costume renderings, watercolor is a versatile paint. Its translucent washes make the paint appealing, but it can also achieve vivid, opaque colors.

Gouache

Gouache is similar to watercolors, but it has extra binders added to make the colors opaquer. This paint also comes in both tubes and pans, though stores commonly sell the tubes. Gouache and watercolors can be mixed together as needed. Gouache is a good choice for costume renderings because of its versatility.

Pastels

Pastels are powdered pigments pressed into sticks and used like crayons. They come in a soft or hard variety. The soft pastels are suitable for coloring in large areas with vivid hues; the harder pastels can be sharpened to a point for detail work. Pastels don't mix in the same way paints do, but to compensate, manufacturers offer hundreds of colors. Pastels emit dust, so they should be used in a well-ventilated area.

Colored Pencils

Colored pencils are inexpensive, accessible, and have a lower learning curve compared to paints. Colored pencils are easy to control. With a sharpened point, a designer can include delicate details without worrying about proper brushes and paint. However, it is more difficult to mix colors and to cover large areas.

Colored pencils have wax or oil as its binder, which resists any color layered on top. Like pastels, mixing colors isn't as easy as paint, but a designer can use tools like paper blending stumps can smooth the colors together.

For a costume rendering, colored pencils make a great choice because they are easy to learn and control. Some brands of colored pencils have over a hundred colors to choose from.

Watercolors, gouache, pastels, and colored pencils can be available in two or three levels—the usual levels are student quality and artist quality. Student-grade has more binder than pigment to keep the cost low, but it also is more challenging to work with and isn't as dynamic. The artist-grade is more expensive, but has superior color quality. For a person who desires a career in costume design, one should practice with the student grade quality, then invest in the higher quality tools when moving into the professional industry.

Collage/Mixed Media

A collage uses found images (such as from magazines or newspapers) that an artist pieces together to create an image. Paint and colored pencils can be used to give the rendering definition. Objects from nature (such as flower petals) can add texture. A designer can lay a foundation in paint, but fill in the details with colored pencil. They can also block in all the colors on a computer, then print on watercolor paper and paint the rest. Collage and mixed media is a freeform style of rendering where the designer finds ideas from the parts and pieces of many things.

Collage works well for designers who enjoy discovery and experimentation. Shapes and textures from found objects can be mixed-and-matched to create exciting combinations.

A collage can be inexpensive, too. Used creatively, found objects such as discarded newspapers, fabric scraps, grocery bags, and many other materials can make interesting textures on a rendering.

DIGITAL MEDIA

Software has given designers a new way to create and share renderings. Paints and pencils have been around for thousands of years, but digital has only been around for decades and changes every month. This can either be a boon to a designer or a source of frustration. As soon as an artist is practiced enough to be comfortable on a platform, the software company may have released a new version with updated features and dozens of new tools. When adopting new versions, an artist does not have to start from the beginning. Old skills, keyboard shortcuts, and general techniques are transferable. A designer may have to get accustomed to a new layout or tool, but given a little time and experimentation, the designer can work their way back to their usual efficiency. Costume designers also don't need all the tools a professional digital artist does. They can ignore many of the features not relevant to their discipline.

Adobe Creative Suite

Adobe develops industry-standard software for artists of all varieties. Adobe Photoshop is an editing software that can be used for painting, photo editing, or both. Adobe hosts dozens of tutorials on its website to help users. Along with Adobe's official tutorials, artists on YouTube have uploaded thousands of tips and tricks for novices and experts. For the individual, Adobe is licensed through a subscription model, paid per month or per year.

For a costume designer, Photoshop's strength is its layer tool. In traditional painting, a mistake may mean a whole rendering needs to be redone completely. In editing software like Photoshop, each step can be drawn and evaluated on their own layers. The base color can be on one layer, the textures on another, and so on. If the results of one layer aren't satisfactory, one can delete it without affecting the rest of the painting.

Photoshop also comes with a variety of other useful tools. Paint brushes, and the ability to design a custom paintbrush, can add unique textures to the rendering. Choosing the perfect color is easy with the eyedropper tool. Masking is a feature that can isolate and edit specific parts of the image. The transformation tool can help alter proportion. Puppet warp can change the positioning of selected parts without affecting the rest of the composition.

Renderings in photoshop aren't foolproof, however. A designer must develop the habit of saving their work often, both on and off the computer. Backups are essential—all too often artists lose their work forever due to a computer malfunction. The risk is lowered if copies of the work are stored on three devices: the computer's hard drive, a cloud service (an Internet-based storage system like Dropbox), and an external storage device. The color on a monitor can also be imprecise. What looks green on one monitor can print out bluer than the designer intended. Different computer monitors, phones, and tablets change the color displayed. If a designer wants to share a rendering with consistent hues, painting with physical media may be the best option.

Adobe Sketch is a mobile application designed to feel more like drawing on natural paper while keeping the advantages of digital work. It can work with special styluses designed to mimic pens, or an artist can draw with the finger. Sketches can be exported to Adobe Illustrator or Photoshop for further editing.

Adobe Capture is a mobile application that is a supplemental tool for artists meant to be combined with other programs like Photoshop or Sketch. Capture can help a designer bring in texture and color from their surroundings. It uses the mobile device's built-in camera to turn photographs into textures for 3D models, into repeating patterns, or into custom brushes for use in Photoshop. Capture can also pick out colors in the environment that can be arranged into a harmonious color scheme. Both Adobe Sketch and Adobe capture are free. If extra storage is needed in the cloud, a per month subscription is available.

Procreate

Procreate is a drawing application for mobile devices. It is a tool the designer can use to sketch and draw with tools that closely mimic drawing on paper. It offers a variety of brushes, the ability to smudge and blend, and has a layers option like Photoshop. Procreate is compatible with the Apple Pencil, which is sensitive to pressures. Files can be exported as a PDF, JPEG, PNG, TIFF, and PSD. The app also allows easy sharing with directors via email. Procreate is an affordable program, but, as of 2019, it is only available in the Apple App store.

3D Modeling

A designer can elect to render a costume in 3D, giving the design team a lifelike idea of what the final product will look like. The designer can provide views of the garment from all angles and give information about the outfit's weight and movement. 3D modelers can use dozens of programs. Highlighted here are two software possibilities.

Marvelous Designer

Marvelous Designer is a software that allows a designer to create and adjust digital clothing patterns, then renders that pattern into a 3D shape on a model. Users can give the program information about the fabric weight and texture, which will automatically adjust the model. This program allows designers to share a full 360-degree view of the costume.

Zbrush

Zbrush is a sculptor's tool. In this program, a designer can take a digital lump of "clay" and carve into it just as a sculptor would do. Designers can add clay, subtract, etch, stipple either freehand, or they can use a symmetry tool that carves equally on both sides of the model. Zbrush is excellent for prosthetic models or creature work, but it can also be used for classic costume design.

CONSIDERING DIFFERENT TYPES OF SPACES

Armed with all the knowledge and information from the script analysis, the costume designer will next translate their ideas into a design. The approach will depend on the story's medium.

Film, theater, and television come with individual challenges and limitations. From open spaces of large operas to the small screens of a phone, each requires different strategies when designing.

High-definition movies and 4K television shows feature the highest amount of resolution for the viewer (4K is a name that refers to the approximately 4000 horizontal pixels on a screen). In this medium, designers can make use of small details and fine textures because high-definition film broadcasts on wide screens with hyper-clarity. In film, the screens can be twelve meters (or forty feet) wide, amplifying stitching lines on clothes, and quality of the material.

While high definition television is ideal for design minutiae, large venues need to be designed on a much bigger scale. Large operas can be performed in houses that can hold more than 3000 people. Concerts play in stadiums that hold 80,000 to a 100,000 people. Unlike the 4K resolution of modern television and cinema, small details are lost in large houses; some so much that people can appear as blobs of color to the furthest member of the crowd. Big spaces and concert venues need a design that is broader and more exaggerated. Eyes would need to be lined in thick black; costumes might be shadowed and highlighted to help decorative elements pop. Edges must be harsher and more clearly defined.

Other types of venues vary in audience orientation and stage depth, all of which a designer will need to adapt to. The following are common types of stages a costume designer will encounter.

Proscenium: Prosceniums are stages that are framed with a square or arch. The audience sits on one side of the arch and the action of the play happens on the other. Behind the arch is a curtain that divides the front of the stage (called the apron) and the main playing area. The space behind the arch out of view of the audience is called the wings.

Thrust Stage: The playing space of a thrust stage juts out into the audience on three sides. The stage is connected to an upstage playing area, which could have a proscenium arch.

Traverse Stage or Alley Stage: Audiences in an alley stage sit on opposing sides of the playing space, typically facing each other. Catwalks are the most commonly encountered alley stage.

Arena, or Theater-in-the-Round: The audience of an arena stage surrounds the playing space on all sides. Usually, scenery is limited in these spaces because tall structures could block the view of the action for some of the audience.

Black Box: The playing space of black box theaters can change based on the show. The configuration of the audience can resemble any of the traditional theater spaces, or it can be arranged into something new.

Amphitheater and other open-air venues: Outdoor theaters can be in any of the above audience configurations, but are exposed to the weather. Some naturally occurring rock formations have been transformed into open-air stages.

Promenade Theater: The audience in a promenade space walks around with the action. This type of theater is commonly more interactive than other theater types.

Film, theater, and television are a costume designer's main creative outlet, but it is not the only way to exercise one's talent. Animation, computer graphics, and video games also need a costume designer's expertise, providing unique challenges not found in any other medium. In theater, a designer can rely upon gravity, space, and air to move the fabric around an actor; but in animation, physics must be created and calculated, then rendered by a massive network of computers. An animator who renders clothing will need to know how fabric drifts, floats, and hangs to create convincing movement— something a costume designer would be intimately familiar with. Without knowing how fabric moves, a cape might end up looking as if it weighs a thousand pounds, or a dress could hang off a character with the flexibility of bricks.

When considering the medium, some designers may tailor their research to their budget; some like to research and design without limitations and adapt afterward. Either approach depends on a designer's individual style, one that is developed after years of trial-and-error.

HOW TO PRESENT IDEAS

A great idea won't get far if the team is unconvinced of its merit. A designer must also develop communication skills so they can effectively promote the design to the team, the director, the producers, and even marketing. However, stage fright can take hold. It is essential to understand that public speaking is a skill that needs to be practiced, just like drawing, painting, sewing. Messing up is not only inevitable, it is expected.

Speaking in front of a crowd, no matter the size, is an exercise in confidence and "reading" the vibe of a room. This is why acting classes are valuable. It teaches the new designer how to separate their sense of personal worth from the anxiety that comes from the fear of messing up in front of people. It "loosens" the pressure that people place upon themselves when they're asked to "perform" in a social environment.

The design team is a group of equals, not a hierarchy. The others are a costume designer's colleagues, even in an academic environment. As a group, the team talks about their ideas while the others help brainstorm. Some thoughts are good, some not so good. A design team that feels comfortable talking to each other in a presentation environment has the best chance of achieving a harmonious design.

A common trap that new designers fall into is excessive apologizing during the presentation.

"I want Beatrice in a red dress. Sorry, the rendering is a little messy, I did it quickly."

"Sorry. The sleeves look big here, sorry. It'll look good on the actress."

An artist's worst critic is themselves. Pointing it out and apologizing only draws attention to what otherwise might have been either overlooked or was never a problem in the first place. Apologizing also assigns a negative framing on the overall presentation. Confidence will always convince the team better than negativity.

An effective presentation requires different strategies based on the audience: Selling an idea to close friends is different than selling one to a legendary director, but a few tips can help in any situation.

Before the meeting, the designer should organize notes. Improvising on the spot can lead to a haphazard delivery that uses up time while only saying a fraction of what needs to be said. A designer who is prepared will be seen as more professional and, therefore, will build trust between colleagues.

Meetings are generally short, sometimes as brief as an hour (unless many complicated elements need discussing). In that time, each designer will need to talk about their ideas. The presentations should be kept succinct. The designers should take no more than ten minutes to articulate their designs for the show. If using a slide presentation software like Microsoft's Powerpoint, a designer should limit themselves to under twenty slides and spend no longer than thirty seconds explaining each one. This forced reduction will help pare down the proposal to its most important pieces.

Brevity is the soul of wit as the character Polonius said in Shakespeare's Hamlet. This means that a concise speech is an effective speech. Useful information can be buried under a long-winded and meandering presentation, but no one will know which point contains the essential parts. When presenting, a designer should focus on the big picture and how it fits in with the overall aesthetic, then talk of the finer points when it is relevant. That is, a designer shouldn't focus on details like "*the blue buttons symbolize her tears.*" If the idea cannot be understood without extensive explanation, then it is not needed. Instead, one should center on the parts that engage the team's interests: "*Her plum-colored dress will contrast against the stark white walls; under the golden light, it will turn a dour gray, emphasizing her mourning.*"

The audience will likely respond better when they are engaged directly rather than being told dry details. Instead of saying, "This is a dress, and the character will have red hair," a designer should show what the design means using images and specific descriptions. Because "red hair" and a "dress" are so vague that they can mean many different things to many different people, it communicates very little. Clarity is the best tool to avoid confusion in the production process. "A person with rust-colored hair wearing a tube-top and mini-skirt" paints a different picture to "A person with dark mahogany hair wearing a silk, jewel-encrusted bias-cut evening gown."

Showing an incomplete picture can also lead to confusion. When explaining the characters in terms of their costume design, it is best to present an image or drawing that matches a designer's ideas. An uncertain designer might say, "*Beatrice will wear a blouse similar to the one pictured, but it'll have different sleeves, be a different color, and have a lower neckline.*" This statement raises more questions than it answers. What kind of sleeves? What color? How low a neckline? After a presentation, the team should know exactly what to expect. A better strategy would be to find an image that portrays precisely what the designer is picturing. If an image cannot be found, then it should be drawn.

Another general statement new designers say is, "*It'll look good from far away.*" This implies that the image shown is not going to be how the final product is perceived. It also makes a promise that is not guaranteed, especially without the context of the sets and lights. It lacks confidence by openly acknowledging that the designer is settling for something below their personal standards. The claim is also unverifiable—will it genuinely look good from far away? The best tactic is to show a garment as it is meant to be perceived.

A designer should make promises that can be kept. It might be easy to say yes to all of the other designer's ideas to seem more collaborative. However, promising something that cannot be done can seriously affect the work of the director, actor, and other designers. It is not unusual for something to come up that needs either research or consultation from the costume shop before a decision can be made. In these situations, the conversation can be tabled for later. It is better to delay a choice than to make a hasty, uninformed one.

Once a designer understands how to communicate their choices, they can edit down until only the vital ideas are left. The rest can be shared in one-on-one conversations with the specific team members that need to know. That way, the overall group gets a summary while the interested parties can schedule as much time as they need to discuss the details.

A designer should communicate where there is flexibility. Sometimes, unexpected obstacles happen in the rehearsal process that might affect the look of the clothes. If there is a moment in the script that could be tricky to execute, talk about different possible options.

SUMMARY

- A design is a compilation of imagery that is communicated through line, texture, shape, and color. Each of these elements is combined to create a moving painting on stage that has energy and emotion.
- Costume design is understanding the appeal of the story from the perspective of the team, the audience, and of the designer themselves.
- Color comes from light. Learning to manipulate this light through value, saturation, and hue can create combinations that communicate emotion.
- A design is presented through renderings, which can be created in a variety of media. It can be in a physical form using watercolor, gouache, colored pencils, collage, or a mixture of all; or, it can be digital using programs such as Adobe Photoshop, Procreate, or Zbrush.
- Designing for various media—whether that is film,

theater, television, animation, or video games—requires different approaches.

- Discussing a design with the team is a practice in public speaking. A concise, pointed presentation will help express a designer's concept quickly and confidently.

4

PREPARING FOR CONSTRUCTION

INTRODUCTION TO THE COSTUME SHOP

Designing costumes requires practice along with ample trial-and-error. While this book can give general advice on a typical production, every costume shop will work differently, and every show will have different needs.

Adapting one's design strategy to best fit with the personality and working style of the shop is advisable. The shops themselves will also be flexible to meet the designer's expectations. Their goals and the designer's goals are the same, both working together to make the best show possible. Collaborative art is a compromise, just as it was in the design phase, and it is no different in the production phase.

Costume shop styles vary. In shops with short turnaround times and small budgets, they may be keen to work with the philosophy of "done is good." In this working style, fixating on flawless accuracy and fine details isn't as crucial as being finished.

Some shops that employ highly skilled labor and have a reputation for producing exquisite work, will favor quality instead of speed and quantity. In order to maintain a fast pace, these shops may employ dozens of employees to produce large amounts of masterful work in a short amount of time.

Most shops exist somewhere in the middle of the spectrum, trying to maintain as high a quality as possible for the time and budget they are given. None of these is the "wrong" approach. Art cannot truly be separated into "right" and "wrong," only "effective for what it's trying to achieve" or "not effective." When figuring out a workplace strategy, a designer and a shop manager should set goals first.

What would the designer like to accomplish? What are the aesthetic expectations of the show? How can it be done within the budgeted time and money? If it can't, could the theater increase the budget?

The perfect balance of understanding and adaptation is a skill that is learned over a whole career; mistakes will inevitably be made. A designer must try new techniques and new collaborations to hone their work style. When the process is both satisfying and rewarding, that is a technique done right.

SHOP PERSONNEL

When the design phase is complete, the designer will start working with an additional team who will realize the costume design into wearable garments.

Costume shops are organized in many ways. Large shops may have dozens of skilled people working in specialist roles. Smaller shops may have one person filling all the jobs. A standard costume shop will have a combination of the following positions:

Costume Shop Manager: The shop manager leads the crew. They're responsible for hiring, keeping budget, drafting schedules, maintaining the build process, requesting overtime, and making sure the shop retains the expected construction quality. The shop manager works closely with the costume designer. They will lead discussions on the practical limitations in the design and adjust the labor and budget accordingly, hiring extra help for a show if needed. They will be familiar with local talent should a specialty artist be required for the production (like a knitter, wig maker, or a welder). If a designer is unfamiliar with the area, a shop manager can recommend places to shop. They may also provide rides to a designer that doesn't have a car.

Assistant Costume Designer: Sometimes shortened to ACD, this person helps the designer with organizational tasks and paperwork. They also aid in keeping the designer organized by taking notes at meetings and fittings. ACDs coordinate costumes that are needed in bulk, like socks and undershirts, and keep track of costume rentals. Each morning when the stage manager sends out a report, an assistant costume designer will respond to rehearsal item request and consult with the designer on any questions raised.

In the absence of an assistant costume designer, these duties may be carried out by the shop manager or the first hand.

ACDs may not be directly employed by the theater, but by the designer themselves. Costume designers and their assistants can become a team that travels and works together.

Draper: The draper is considered the lead on costume construction. They are responsible for figuring out the best way to build the designer's costumes. They begin by draping fabric onto a dress form and sculpting it until it matches the renderings. In this stage, the draper may seek approval from the designer, especially if the garment is complicated. From there, the draper takes the fabric off the dress form and uses the pieces to create a paper pattern that others will use to construct the garment.

Throughout the process, the designer will consult with the draper about construction details of a garment and the fit on an actor's body. The art of draping is intricately linked together with the art of costume design. A draper must use their design knowledge to interpret the costume research renderings and translate them into garments that fit.

Working with the draper is crucial in transitioning a design from the page to the stage. A costume rendering may look beautiful as a painting on watercolor paper, but if the costume doesn't look good on the actor, then the design won't achieve what it was meant to do.

If a theater does not employ a draper, the duties may fall to the costume shop manager or the designer.

First Hand: A first hand is a draper's assistant. They help correct **patterns** (blueprints used to construct a garment) and often do the **cutting**. In simple terms, *cutting* refers to cutting pieces of the costume out of fabric, but the actual task is complicated and requires a high level of precision to master. Cutting requires the first hand to match patterns and line up the grain—a task exponentially more difficult for silky or slippery fabrics like chiffon.

A first hand instructs the stitchers about the built garments. They also organize the alterations and assist in fittings.

Should a theater not employ a first hand, the duties may be carried out by the draper.

Stitcher: Stitchers are masters of hand stitching and the machine. They are the primary constructor of the costumes and sew the majority of the alterations. Some are experienced in other needle arts such as embroidery and knitting.

Costume Crafts: A costume craftsperson is in charge of creating accessories like crowns, jewelry, and shoes. They also dye fabric, distress garments, create armor, create masks, or do special painting on costumes. Any costume creation task that isn't stitching may fall under costume crafts.

Wardrobe Supervisor: Wardrobe supervisors are in charge of running the show from **dress rehearsals** (a set of practice runs near the end of the production process where the actors wear the costumes on set) to closing night. A wardrobe supervisor creates paperwork that plots their crews' actions through the course of the show. They also organize quick-change strategies. After opening, the wardrobe supervisor is in charge of maintaining the quality of the costumes by making repairs and overseeing laundry.

Dresser: A dresser is under the supervision of the wardrobe supervisor. They make sure all costume pieces are cleaned, organized, and in their proper place. Dressers help the actors into their costume, especially if the garment is complicated. Dressers will also **preset** costumes that are involved in quick changes. While the performance is running, a dresser maintains the looks of the actor exactly as the designer intends. That means a dresser must straighten ties, smooth skirts, lint-roll jackets, or comb back frazzled hair before an actor make their entrance. If a separate laundry position is not available, the dressers will be in charge of washing the clothes.

If the theater does not employ a dresser, a wardrobe supervisor will act as the lone person on the crew. In small theaters with neither dressers nor wardrobe supervisors, actors themselves have been known to be each other's dressers.

Wigs: Sometimes known as a wig master, this person is in charge of ventilating wigs (which is a construction method where each strand of hair is hand-tied). They also cut and style the hair. A wig master may be in charge of maintaining the hair style during the run of the show, but if they aren't present, then the responsibility moves to the dressers.

Tailor: Tailors specialize in menswear, but they can also build structured women's garments, like a pants suit. Menswear requires different construction techniques than their dressmaker counterparts, so specialists are usually hired if a suit needs constructed.

Dyers: Dyers are responsible for custom dying fabric. They keep notebooks full of recipes and formulas that record how dyes chemically react with many types of material. They are masters of color, for they often have to precisely match skin tones or recreate color swatches the designer provides.

For shops without dedicated dyers, the duties fall to the craftsperson.

Milliners: This position in the costume shop is specifically for hat-making or any other accessory worn on the head. Milliners are skilled in shaping felt over wooden blocks into top hats, fedoras, derbies, homburgs, and many others. They can also build extravagant headdresses from wire, fabric, and thermoplastics. A milliner must have a strong knowledge of materials; large hats need to be kept light so as not to strain the actor's spine.

A theater without a milliner may assign the duties to a craftsperson.

Rental/Stock Manager: This position is in charge of organizing and cataloging the costume stock, and helps designers find what is needed. Rental managers bring in additional revenue by renting costumes to other theaters and local groups.

If a theater doesn't have a rental manager on staff, the shop manager or the assistant can fill the role.

Interns: Interns can encompass many roles depending on the theater. They're often students in high school or college that are learning the craft. They may act as stitchers, design assistants, dressers, or be all three.

Overhire: Overhire isn't a position with a set role; they can contribute to the show with any of the skills listed above. The difference is that an overhire position is employed on a situational basis. A shop manager may determine that a musical needs four stitchers, but the theater may only employ two permanently. In these situations, the shop manager can hire local talent for that one show.

Specialty Positions and Outsourcing: Many staff positions may only be needed for specific situations. Hiring a full-time knitter or embroiderer may not make economic sense, but they can be commissioned for particular shows that need it. A costume shop manager will determine if the budget will allow for a specialty position to be hired.

Stitching jobs can also be outsourced if the in-house costume shop can't accomplish the necessary construction in the time allotted.

A costume designer may not directly collaborate with many of these positions, but they all work together to fulfill the designer's vision. Each of them has their areas of expertise that can be consulted to solve problems. They'll know all about practical limitations and the creative methods available to fix them. A designer should listen to their input, then consider if the feedback is applicable.

The shop positions depend on the scope of the theater. Very few save for the largest theater will employ all the jobs listed above. An average-sized theater may only have a shop manager, a draper, a first hand, and a few stitchers. A small theater may only have a shop manager and an intern. A startup theater with minimal funds might require the designer themselves to fulfill all the roles. The scale of the build and level of detail will increase with a more extensive shop. The biggest costume houses may have the skill, budget, and labor to construct every costume from scratch. Medium range theaters will need to split that labor between building and alterations. A small theater may not be able to build anything, working only from stock and rentals.

Regardless of the situation, a designer must be flexible and adapt to their working environment.

COSTUME SHOP TOOLS

The costume shop has its own specialized set of tools. A designer does not need to master the art of sewing, but they should be familiar with how a basic garment is put together. The more knowledge they have in construction techniques, the easier it will be to have a conversation with the people that build their design.

Needles: Needles are metal pins that are sharp on one end and have an eye on the other. Each size and shape serves a different purpose. Average sewing needles come in an assortment of lengths and are sharp enough to go through the majority of fabrics used in garment making. Mattress needles are long (around seven inches) and are designed to travel through thick material. Tapestry needles are usually blunt and have a large eye to accommodate thick yarns. Curved needles are useful in upholstery or millinery work. They are suitable for sewing inflexible material. Leather needles have a sharp, flat tip that's designed to pierce tough buckskin or suede. Beading needles have a long, thin shaft and are used in delicate beadwork.

Sewing Machine: Sewing machine inventors in the nineteenth century sought to replace the old hand sewing methods by automating the process with the lockstitch. A modern, basic sewing machine can do straight stitching and zig-zag stitching, along with some decorative and specialty sewing.

Serger: Sergers are machines that use three or four threads to bind edges of fabric to prevent fraying.

Iron: A machine that uses heat and steam to flatten out wrinkles in clothes. Initially, it was a piece of cast iron that was heated on a fire. Today, machines are electric and come in a domestic variety for use at home or an industrial style used in commercial industries.

Thread: Spun fiber that is used to sew cloth together.

Picker or Seam Ripper: A small blade that is used to take garments apart by "picking" the thread of a sewn seam.

Safety Pins: A pin that is capped with a smooth head to prevent poking.

Mannequin or Dress Form: A dummy that is a representation of the human body. A draper pins fabric on a mannequin to sculpt costumes before translating it into a pattern. Dress forms can also be used to display garments.

Shears or Scissors: A tool used to cut. Dressmaker's shears can be heavy, long, and sharp; they should be used for fabric only. Snips (or nippers) are short scissors used to cut thread. Applique shears are designed for a controlled cut when fabric needs to be trimmed close to a seam. Pinking shears cut fabric in a zig-zag pattern and are used to prevent fraying.

Rulers: Used in pattern making to create precise lines and measurements. Tape measures are soft and flexible and are ideal for taking body measurements. French curves and hip curves help a draper or a first hand draw smooth lines on a pattern. Clear plastic rules help measure seam allowances.

Racks: Stands or rods where costumes are organized and hung.

Steamer: A machine with a water tank that heats up and billows steam out of a long wand. Steamers are good at releasing wrinkles from fabrics that can't be ironed. It can also re-awaken garments that have been crushed in storage or heat-set fabrics that have been dyed.

Tailor's Chalk: Chalk that is used to mark on fabric. Over time, the mark wears away.

Twill Tape: A ribbon made with the twill weave; its strength is useful when stabilizing fabrics or providing backing for snaps or buttons.

Bias Tape: Ribbon created from the bias of fabric. Bias can gracefully bend around curved seams.

·**Thimbles**: Protects the stitcher's fingers from the sharp end of pins and needles, usually made from metal, leather, or plastic.

THE STAGE MANAGER

A stage manager supervises rehearsals and assists the director. They are the keeper of schedules and the main production organizer. For a costume designer, the stage manager is the liaison between the shop and the actors.

During the design phase, a stage manager will record detailed meeting notes for the designers to review and reference. Each report should be thoroughly read; any information that is either incorrect or incomplete should be communicated to the stage manager so the record can be updated. A stage manager's paperwork is considered the "official" account. If there are ambiguities or misunderstandings between two members of the team, the designers can refer to the stage manager's paperwork for clarification. For example, the set designer might think the overall color scheme of a show would be "blue," but the costume designer heard "yellow." If neither can recall what the team decided upon, the stage manager's notes should say if a consensus was reached. If not, the team may require another meeting. This is why it is essential to check that the stage manager's notes reflect the designer's ideas. If the report says, "all parties agreed on blue," it would be difficult for a designer to contradict it.

A designer should always request fittings through the stage manager, who can can shift the schedule around so that the costume designers get the fitting time they require. Some equity rules limit the number of times an actor can be called for a fitting, and there may be limits regarding the duration. A stage manager will have that information and relay it to the costume shop.

A stage manager records information from rehearsals into an email called the **rehearsal report**. This document updates the team about the show's progress and communicates essential information. For a costume designer, a rehearsal report will contain the fitting schedule and rehearsal item requests along with any relevant questions and ideas.

When reading a rehearsal report, a designer should read all sections, including the notes in other tech categories. Since all areas of design are interlinked, a change in one area can affect another area. In the following hypothetical rehearsal report in Figure 4.1, the notes in each field contain information that would affect costumes. In this scenario, a designer would need to inquire about a twisted ankle

Page 1 of 1
Director: M. Smith
SM: E. Stafford
ASM: C. Dawson

Rehearsal Report #1
Date: 5/14/19
Location: Antionette Falbo Theatre, CAC rm. 1512

Attendance:	
Rehearsed:	
Accidents/Injuries:	Jose Garcia twisted his ankle

NOTES:	
General:	None, thank you.
Director:	None, thank you.
Lights:	None, thank you.
Sound:	None, thank you.
Scenery:	Can we have three candles for the dinner table in the final scene?
Technical:	None, thank you.
Costumes:	1. Hero was wondering if she had a pocket to store her apple?
Props:	Director would like to talk about the barbecue wings in the Party Scene
Fight Choreo.:	None, thank you.
Stage Mgt.:	None, thank you.
Prod. Mgt.:	None, thank you.
Voice/Dialect:	None, thank you.
Script:	None, thank you.

Costume Fittings:				
Monday, May 13	Tuesday, May 14	Wednesday, May 15	Thursday, May 16	Friday, May 17

FIGURE 4.1 An example of a typical rehearsal report. Paperwork courtesy of Emily Stafford.

note. Will the actor be replaced? If they aren't, will they have a medical brace that needs to be accommodated? Will he need any special assistance changing?

In the props section, the report notes that barbecue wings will be added to the scene. Is this real food? Food can be messy, which can be problematic around costumes that are dry-clean only. The note in the costumes section about the food in Hero's pocket seems to refer to the barbecue wings in the props section. If this action is needed, it might necessitate that the actor's pockets are lined in plastic that will need to be replaced every night. The cleaning budget may also need to be increased.

Under the set section, the notes mention a candle. Depending on the local laws, this may indicate that the costumes need fireproofed, which may require a budget increase depending on the number of costumes exposed. In addition, it may be wise to remove any polyester fabrics near the flame. Polyester melts when on fire, and if that melted fabric sticks to an actor, it could cause serious injury. A discussion should happen between the technical director and the fire marshal regarding any live flame on the set.

A stage manager is also knowledgeable in Actor's Equity contracts (a professional actors' union). Along with the costume shop manager, a designer will have to plan to accommodate the needs in the agreement. This may mean calling an actor for fittings no more than two times. This rule is to prevent a costume designer from calling an actor for an excessive number of fittings, taking them away from needed rehearsal time. A costume designer should be organized; inefficiency can impact the productivity of the actor as well as the shop itself. A later section will explain other common considerations in an Actor's Equity contract.

When in doubt about who to approach for any problem, the stage manager is an appropriate person to contact first. If they cannot help solve an issue, they may be able to point the designer to the right place.

THE PRODUCTION CALENDAR

The stage manager will operate under a master schedule called the production calendar. This document contains all design meetings, rehearsals, production meetings, designer run-throughs, technical

SUMMER 2020
PRODUCTION CALENDAR

Page 1 of 2
9/10/19 ees
Version: DRAFT
PM: E. Stafford

Figure 4.2   An example of a typical rehearsal schedule. Paperwork courtesy of Emily Stafford.

rehearsals, and any other dates of interest, pictured in Figure 4.2. From that paperwork, a designer can use the schedule to plan a course of action. Designers can collaborate with costume shop managers and plan a to-do list that can be used to prioritize tasks, such as the day all the fabric needs to be in the shop, the due date for all the trims, the best day to travel to rental houses, and when fittings can happen. In academia, a production calendar may also list student activities and obligations, such as finals week.

THE PIECE LIST

Once the director approves the renderings, a designer creates a **piece list**. A piece list is a document that lists everything an actor wears in the show (including incidentals like socks and undershirts) divided by character and scene. It is the master database that serves as a source for most of the other paperwork the designer needs to produce. It also acts as a checklist for the designer and the costume shop manager so that each item can be tracked, as shown in Figure 4.3.

To make a piece list, a designer lists every character and writes down every costume item they wear, starting with what touches the

Scene/ Character	Items	Obtained	Scene/ Character	Items	Obtained
Act I Scene 1	black socks		Act II Scene 1		
Street Salesman	work shoes	✓	Butler	black socks	✓
	work pants	✓		black tuxedo pants	✓
	undershirt	✓		black dress shoes	
	white dress shirt	✓		cummerbund	✓
	apron	✓		black jacket	✓
	neckerchief	✓		white gloves	✓
	gloves	✓		bowtie	
	newsboy cap	✓		ring	✓
Act I Scene 2				white tuxedo shirt	✓
Butler	black socks	✓	Act II Scene 2		
	black tuxedo pants	✓	Party Guest	white socks	✓
	black dress shoes	✓		white tuxedo pants	✓
	cummerbund	✓		blue tuxedo shirt	
	black jacket	✓		violet damask vest front	✓
	white gloves			white dinner jacket	✓
	bowtie	✓		white top hat	✓
	ring	✓			
	white tuxedo shirt	✓			

Figure 4.3 An example of a costume piece list.

skin first: boxers, socks, tights, bras, chemises, undershirts, corsets, etc. Each layer on top of the undergarments is listed next: pants, skirts, blouses, waistcoats. After recording the clothing pieces, the accessories would be next: rings, necklaces, earrings, satchels, ties, shoes, watches, and glasses. Finally, one should list the hair and makeup items: wigs, fascinator, barrettes, latex nose application, and fake scar.

The piece list can be altered for many purposes. Formatted as a checklist, it allows the designer to see at a glance how much of the show still needs pulled, rented, or bought. It also helps the designer and the shop manager make sure nothing is forgotten.

Piece lists can also be split into four subcategories: The "buy list," which compiles the costumes that need to be bought either online or in a store; the "rent list," which are costumes that can be rented from costume houses or other theaters; the "pull list," which are costumes that can be found in the theater's own stock; and the "build list," which lists all the costumes being constructed, whether in-house or outsourced. These lists are invaluable to a costume shop manager, who will use it to organize labor and develop a precise budget.

The piece list can be further compartmentalized into more and more specific categories depending on the costume designer's needs. A designer might want to make a list of all the men's white button-down shirts sorted by size so an assistant or an intern can pull these items efficiently. Or, a designer might want to list all the shoes if they need to go shopping. This minute-detail style of paperwork isn't always required, but it can increase the effectiveness of a shop, especially on shows with a lot of costumes.

Once the show moves into technical rehearsals, the piece list aids the wardrobe crew and the actors. Each actor will need a meticulous table of all the costume pieces they wear, when they wear it, when they change, and where they change. To create this chart, a costume designer can combine the information on the piece list with the information on the costume plot. The wardrobe manager will then transfer the information and make a **quick-change** plot and organize the crew's actions during the show.

Creative and skillful shopping is a designer's best weapon. The internet has provided more resources than ever before, but, when shopping, a designer must navigate it with caution, just as they did in the research phase.

WHAT MEASUREMENTS MEAN AND HOW A DESIGNER CAN USE THEM

The measurement sheet is a table that records all of an actor's sizes and proportions. Each costume shop usually has a customized version developed to suit their working style. A concise measurement sheet may only have basic store sizing. Exhaustive measurement sheets cover everything from an actor's shoulder blade width to their foot circumference (Figure 4.4). A designer may not need to reference comprehensive measurements; they are intended more for a draper to draft patterns. However, a designer can use the shop's in-house measurement sheet to create an abridged version for pulling and shopping purposes.

The abridged version of the measurement sheet is called a **cheat sheet**. Cheat sheets are organized in a table that can be referenced quickly. It is easier to take a single-paged cheat sheet to a store than it is to carry a binder.

School of Theatre Measurements		Date Updated:	
Name:		Shoe:	
		Bra:	
Phone:		Dress:	
Email:		Ring:	
Show/ Role:		Leotard:	
Hair cut:		L/R Handed:	
Hair Color/ Dye:		Glasses/ Contacts:	
Height:		Allergies	
Weight:			
Tattoos:		Fitting Considerations:	
Piercings:			

Circumference:				**Back:**			
High neck:				CB neck to shldr blde		to waist:	
Base of Neck				CB neck to floor			
Bust				Shldr/N to princess			
Underbust				Shldr pitch to waist			
Waist				Shldr to Shldr			
High Hip		@		Back neck width		height:	
Hip (fullest):		@		Armscye to Armscye			
Front:				Chest width SS to SS			
CF neck to high bust:		to bust level:		waist width SS to SS			
CF neck to waist:		to floor:		Hip width SS to SS			
Sh/N to Princess:				**Arms:**			
Shldr pitch to Waist:				Shoulder seam:			
point to point:				Nape to shoulder:		to elbow:	
Shldr to shldr:				Nape to wrist:			
Armscye to Armscye:				Shldr bone to elbow:		to wrist:	
Front neck width:		Height:		Underarm to elbow:		to wrist:	
Chest width SS to SS:				Cap height:			
Waist width SS to SS:				Armscye		Bicep:	
Hip width SS to SS:				Elbow:		Forearm:	
Side seam:				Wrist:			
Leg:				**Leg continued:**			
Waist to knee:				Half Girth:		Full girth:	
Waist to ankle (outseam)		to floor:		Thigh:			
Inseam:		to knee:		Knee circumferance:			
Crotch depth: (Chair)				Calf:			
				ankle:			

FIGURE 4.4 An example of a measurement sheet.

The following are common measurements useful to a designer. When browsing stock or shopping in a store, a designer can use these measurements to check a garment's potential fit.

Chest Circumference: This measurement, along with the waist and hip circumference, records the horizontal sizing of a human torso. The chest circumference should be taken just under the armpit or around the peak of the bust point, whichever is fullest. The chest circumference is useful when buying or pulling suits, blouses, bras, and shirts.

Waist Circumference: The waist measurement is taken where the body creases when an actor bends left or right. This is called the **natural waist**, the baseline measurement for the torso. The placement of the waist varies depending on the period. The Regency era England (1811–1820) was a **high-waist** era, sometimes called the **empire waist**. The midsection of dresses in this era sat just under the bust. The early 2000s was a **low-waist** era, with pants and jeans typically sitting just on the hip bone. The waist measurement is useful when buying or pulling dresses or trousers.

Hip Circumference: The hip circumference is taken in two places: high hip and low hip. The high hip is taken near the hip bone, 3 to 5 inches (8 to 13 cm) below the waist, useful for measuring trousers with a low **rise**. A trousers' *rise* describes the distance between the crotch seam and the waist. The longer the rise, the higher the trousers sit on the waist. The shorter the rise, the lower it sits.

The low hip is taken around the fullest part of the hip, 9 to 11 inches below the waist (23 to 28 cm). This measurement is useful for checking to see if a pair of trousers has enough room in the hip area, and for tightly fitted skirts.

Shoulder Width (or "shoulder to shoulder"): This measures the broadness of an actor's back, taken from the bony point of a shoulder to the other shoulder. The shoulder width is more difficult to fit than the chest or waist. Even if the chest size of a garment matches the measurement of an actor, the garment may not be cut to accommodate a full breadth of the shoulders. A designer can check the shoulder width of a garment (like a suit jacket) by placing the measurement tape at the point of the shoulder and measuring across the back, just under the nape of the neck as shown in Figure 4.5.

Height/Weight: These measurements are a quick reference. Suits are sometimes labeled "38L" or "40S," meaning a "long, 38-inch chest size" or a "short, 40-inch chest." Average heights can generally wear standard lengths, but measurements should always be checked. The weight measurement is similar, with the number best used for generalizations instead of specifics. The number doesn't say much about the shape of a person—two people of the same weight can

Figure 4.5 How to take a shoulder-to-shoulder measurement on a suit.

wear drastically different sizes. It can give a general idea, especially for garments not meant to be fitted, like t-shirts.

READING STORE SIZES AND MEASUREMENTS

Knowing the store sizes of an actor can give the designer a starting point when pulling or shopping. This will help a designer narrow down choice. Once they choose a reasonable range of sizes, they can measure the garment and record which might be a better fit. Sizes can vary by store, but there are a few conventions that manufacturers follow.

Shirt Size: For feminine blouses and shirts, manufacturers generally use *small, medium, large, x-large*, sizing labels. There is no standard measurement for what defines "large" or "small." Every company uses its own system. This information gives a general idea of what the actor buys when they shop for themselves, which can help in online purchasing. Otherwise, in a physical store, a designer should measure the garment to see if it would suit the actor's chest circumference, shoulder width, and sleeve length.

Masculine shirts are commonly labeled using the neck size and the sleeve length, displayed with a slash in between: *17/34, 15/32*. For proper shirt measurements, the necks should be measured around the base where the collar would naturally sit. The sleeve should be measured starting at the nape of the neck, then moving to the shoulder, then to the elbow, and finally to the wrist.

Pants Size: For feminine cut pants, sizing can start at 000 and count upwards indefinitely. Like shirts, there are no measurement standards between companies, so the number acts as a reference. The hip circumference and the waist circumference measurement as mentioned is useful to have when shopping in a store.

For masculine cut pants, the sizes displayed are the waist size and the inseam (the number that measures the inside of the leg, running from the crotch to the foot): *34/33, 40/32*. However, the waist size on the label may not correspond directly with an actor's measured size. **Vanity sizing** (a marketing tactic that assigns small numbers to sizes as a way to encourage sales) affects many brands. It is not exclusive to fashion targeting women. Just like when shopping for feminine clothes, measuring the garment is the best way to ensure fit. For online purchases, some websites offer measurement charts, though the numbers are not always accurate. The product reviews usually report whether the sizing of a garment is true to the label.

When pulling or shopping, finding clothes that fit an actor's exact measurements is rare. The best strategy is to buy for the largest part of a person and tailor in the rest. If the hips of a pair of pants fit, it is not uncommon for the waist to be too big. Taking in a garment is generally simpler than letting seams out, especially for commercially manufactured clothes.

Shoe Size: Shoe sizes are more standardized than shirts or pants, but there are variations among manufacturers, especially between shoe types (for example, a pair of stiletto heels fit differently than running shoes). The following describes how the system generally works in the United States, the United Kingdom, and in Europe.

The United States goes by a set of ranges that start at the number label 1 for infants and go up to a toddler size 13.5. This numbering convention is the same for all genders. After 13.5, the shoe sizes restart at size 1, meant for older toddlers (sometimes labeled "big kids 1" to differentiate it from "infant size 1"). For shoes marketed to men, the numbers go up sequentially from there, with no definitive line that separates boys' shoes from men's shoes. For shoes marketed to women, the number system diverges at size "big kids 1." A woman's size 3 overlaps with a "big kids" size 1 and both run in parallel indefinitely. To find the women's size equivalent of a "big kids" shoe, subtract 2 from the adult size: A woman's size 7 is the same as a children's size 5. To find a woman's equivalent size in men's style, add 1.5: A woman's size 8.5 is the same as a men's size 7.

The United Kingdom uses a similar numerical system. Kids sizes start at 0 and number up sequentially to 13.5 before resetting to 1 for "big kids." Though it seems identical to the US, UK sizes and US sizes aren't interchangeable. The most significant difference is that the US system starts the numbering at 1, while the UK system begins at 0.

The European shoe sizing system uses a standardized sizing system for both children and adults, masculine and feminine shoes. They are measured in what's called "Paris Points," which are 2/3 of a centimeter. The sizing in stores generally starts around 15 for infants and is numbered sequentially up from there.

Like clothing, manufacturers will have variations in their sizing. The width of the foot comes with its own standard—some countries denote width in letters, some in numbers. If a designer is unsure about the meaning of shoe sizing labels, websites that sell shoes may provide a conversion chart. Unfortunately, even with a table, ordering shoes online can feel like a guessing game. Designers typically order the same shoe in many sizes—the actor's stated size along with two sizes down and two sizes up—and return what doesn't fit. This works best with retailers that have a "free shipping both ways" policy.

Knowing the complex shoe sizing system of many countries is helpful because casting can vary among ages and genders—and the perfect shoe may not be from one's country of origin. A woman may be cast a young boy and need a pair of boy's shoes, or a man may be cast as an older woman. If a designer is familiar with shoe sizing charts, they can search for appropriate styles for the character while buying the right size for the actor.

Other Measurement Sheet Information: Apart from numerical measurements, a designer may need to know other kinds of information about the actor relevant to costumes.

Contact Information: Usually, a designer will go through the stage manager to contact an actor, but sometimes urgency is needed. The shop personnel may need to contact the actor directly. It is good to have them on file just in case.

Tattoos and Piercings (and a description of where they are on the body): Should an actor have a visible tattoo where their character would not, a designer will need to purchase tattoo concealer to last the duration of the run. The designer can use the actor's piercings. If not, they may need to be covered with a flesh-toned bandage. This technique does not work for hi-definition film or television, so other methods may be required.

Allergies: This information refers to an actor's contact allergies. Latex, wools, dyes, detergents, metals, are common materials in a costume that could be an allergen trigger. If an actor has one of these allergies, an alternative must be found. Surgical-grade stainless steel jewelry is a good alternative to those with nickel allergies. Detergents marked "free and clear" are also gentler on the skin.

Even though ingested allergies aren't usually relevant, there are some specific situations where it might come up. Edible blood packs can be made of corn syrup, chocolate, peanut butter, corn starch, and other various food items. If a situation in a play requires an actor to have something in their mouth, it's best to know any specific food allergies—peanuts, gluten, dairy, etc.

Fitting Considerations: This is a miscellaneous space for an actor to communicate anything that might affect how they wear their costume. This could be an insulin pump that might affect tight-fitting clothing, or it could be a sensory sensitivity to itchy fabrics or labels. An actor's considerations and boundaries should be respected even if it requires a redesign of a character. An actor will trust the designer more if they feel their needs are adequately considered.

BUDGET

In a more extensive shop, the shop manager and the assistant costume designer will be tasked with organizing the budget paperwork. However, in many situations where the staff is limited, a designer will be the only person tracking the expenditures. Knowing how to make suitable paperwork will prevent a designer from either overspending or underspending. A designer should work within their means, but not be afraid to spend what is given to them.

A designer can begin budgeting by using their build/buy/rent document from the piece list. This gives the designer a snapshot view of projected expenses. Once spending begins, a designer should record each item, how much the item cost, and where the item was purchased. This strategy helps not only to keep track of where the money is spent but also can be referred to if duplicate items are needed. Need more fabric? The record will show where it was purchased and for how much. This prevents frantic searching through piles of receipts if there are last-minute changes.

The information on a budget sheet should be organized in an easily readable way. Figure 4.6 is a typical format a designer can utilize. Programs such as Microsoft Excel or Google Docs can create tables with a simple sum function that automatically totals all costs inputted into the fields.

SHOULD THE COSTUMES BE PULLED, PURCHASED OR BUILT?

Budget, time, and labor limit all costumers in some way—even big-budget Hollywood films. When planning the build, a designer determines what is built, what is pulled, what is bought, and what is rented. Much of this strategy is based on budget and shop size, but there are approaches a designer can take based on their own aesthetic.

Utilizing the theater's costume stock is free for the designer. It the most cost-effective place to start. Using stock is great for filling out standard costume items like shirts, pants, skirts, and blouses. A designer can also pull costumes that can be creatively altered and trimmed to match the renderings. Once a designer pulls all they can from stock, they can consider purchasing, renting, or building what is left. For shows with a minimal budget an entire show might be worked from stock.

After consultation with the shop manager, the designer can discuss which costumes they'd like built. Lead characters need the most detail and coordination with the set. Thus, the main characters' costumes are usually the first to be added to a build list. In certain situations,

Item	Character/ Actor	Size	Price	Store
White Shirt	Romeo/ Li	17/35	$19.99	Macy's
White Shirt	Mercutio/ Zhang	15/33	$19.99	Macy's
White shirt	Benvolio/ Gruber	16/33	$19.99	Macy's
Green/ Red plaid shirt	Servant/ Fischer	17/33	$39.50	Nordstrom
Brown pants	Romeo/ Li	34/34	$98.98	Nordstrom
Tan pants	Benvolio/ Gruber	37/32	$43.98	Nordstrom
Tuxedo Pants	Romeo/ Li	34/34	$239.99	Men's Wearhouse
Tuxedo Pants	Benvolio/ Gruber	37/32	$239.99	Men's Wearhouse
Tuxedo Pants	Mercutio/ Zhang	29/28	$239.99	Men's Wearhouse
Orange waistcoat	Servant/ Horvat	L	$49.95	Historical Emporium
Red striped waistcoat	Street Gang/ Jansen	M	$49.95	Historical Emporium
tuxedo shirt	Lord Capulet/ González	16/33	$39.99	Men's Wearhouse
tuxedo shirt	Lord Montague/ Rojas	18/35	$39.99	Men's Wearhouse
Red short skirt	Juliet/ Vera	M	$12.95	Amazon
Blue circle shirt	Juliet's Handmaid/ Flores	L	$19.99	Amazon
Eyelet blouse	Juliet/ Vera	L	$17.99	Amazon
Diamond necklace	Lady Capulet/ Gutierrez	n/a	$260.00	Etsy
Blue prom gown	Ball Attendee/ Wilson	8	$99.99	Sheri's Boutique
Green prom grown	Ball Attendee/ Martin	22	$99.99	Sheri's Boutique
Red prom grown	Ball Attendee/ Sanders	18	$99.99	Sheri's Boutique
Orange prom gown	Ball Attendee/ Barnes	6	$99.99	Sheri's Boutique
Ballroom shoes	Ball Attendee/ Guitierrez	8.5	$225.00	Zappos
Ballroom shoes	Ball Attendee/ Wilson	7.5	$225.00	Zappos
Ballroom shoes	Ball Attendee/ Martin	11	$225.00	Zappos
Ballroom shoes	Ball Attendee/ Sanders	6	$225.00	Zappos
Tennis shoes	Romeo/ Li	11	$68.00	Target
Men's dress shoes	Romeo/ Li	11	$19.99	Target
Men's dress shoes	Benvolio/ Gruber	7	$19.99	Target
Men's dress shoes	Mercutio/ Zhang	9	$19.99	Target
		Total:	$2,881.14	

FIGURE 4.6 An example of a costume budget sheet.

with limited resources, a designer may want to pull or buy the lead characters' costumes in favor of building the chorus. Choruses need to work as a unit. If this group is part of a dance line, they may need matching outfits, which can be challenging to buy or rent, especially if the actors' sizes vary widely. If a shop has a limited amount of labor to use for builds, the chorus may need it more than the leads.

If a script requires a specific style of garment, or if it needs to perform a "trick," that costume would also be a candidate for building. A garment may also need to be added to the build list if the costume stock doesn't have the size and style needed.

A designer and shop manager should budget the cost of materials and labor versus the cost of buying from a store. In the following hypothetical scenario, an average-sized men's white dress shirt can be purchased from a middle-range quality department store for a price between $30 and $80. The fabric for that shirt may cost between $20 and $60 per yard depending on the quality of the material. It may take a stitcher up to ten hours to construct. If that stitcher is paid $16 an hour, the total cost of the built shirt would be between $160 and $500. For cost and time savings, purchasing this garment is most efficient, especially with a limited budget. That time and money could be spent on other costumes that are harder to find. However, situations exist where a designer may deem it necessary to build a commonly found garment. The script might require a specific cut, pattern, or color that is not available in stores. Or, a designer might have found the perfect fabric for the character. Resources are finite no matter how big the budget; the team must decide on how those resources are best spent.

Much of the build/buy list is dependent on the situation, context, and common sense. It can take years to gain a general insight into the shop workload, but a designer isn't alone. Theater, film, and other media are collaborative in more ways than just between designers and directors. Together, the team should be able to create a plan that maximizes aesthetic appeal and the balance of cost and labor.

MEETING WITH THE DRAPER

The draper is in charge of creating patterns for the show's builds and upkeeping the quality of the construction. Before a show moves into the costume shop, the costume designer should provide the draper and the shop manager with a list of builds along with photocopies of all the renderings, supplemental research, and the piece list. Some drapers want the renderings of the items being built, but some like to have all of them, even the ones that will be pulled, rented, or bought. A draper will need to know the overall aesthetic to make informed decisions about the construction. Each draper has their own style of working. Some may want more information; some think less is better. The shop manager and the designer should both meet with the draper and give them the information they need to get started.

When meeting a draper for the first time, a designer should be prepared to answer questions about specific details. The draper may have research of their own that they bring into the discussion.

Undergarments are a necessary part of the discussion, for they are what create a silhouette. Corsets, panniers, and body padding change a person's usual figure, which affects how a costume is draped. Even garments such as push-up bras, sports bras, or hip padding can be enough to alter the fit of a garment. The draper and the designer can collaborate on what undergarments are needed to make the correct costume shapes.

The draper will also need to know details like seam placement. Abstract renderings and gesture drawings may give the director an idea about the intended mood and atmosphere, but a draper needs more concrete information (see Figure 4.7).

If the designer's renderings are stylized, as the one pictured above, a draper may have questions about proportion. Taken literally, some

Figure 4.7 A stylized costume rendering that portrays a distinct mood.

fashionable renderings depict a model that seems eight feet tall with an 18-inch waist. A draper's task is to make the design look just as good on an actor as it does on the exaggerated drawing. A draper could suggest changes that would help the silhouette look more complimentary on the actor. It might be as simple as changing the shape of the neckline, dropping the waist, or changing the direction of stripes. The designer is not obligated to take the suggestion, but they will want to weigh and consider the advice before choosing to either accept or discard it.

Seam lines are another point of interest for a draper. Consider the drawing in Figure 4.8. The drawing gives basic information about the silhouette, but it doesn't provide adequate information for construction. Does the neckline lay at the collarbone, or lower? To some designers it may not matter, but the placement of seams can alter the energy of a garment and affect the proportion of the body. For example, with a strategically placed line, a torso can be made to look longer or shorter. Waists can also be made to look smaller or larger. Shoulders can be broadened.

Figure 4.8 A costume sketch with simple lines but little detail.

Figure 4.9 pictures a complete rendering accompanied by research, inspiration, and notes. The drawing is clear enough to give specific information about silhouette, the flow of the fabric, and details that affect the construction. This package of materials gives the draper enough information to realize the design as intended.

If a designer has specific ideas about the construction, it should be clearly explained to the draper or noted in the rendering or the research. If the designer has no opinions on details, they may leave seam lines and proportions up to the draper. The amount of control a designer wants to maintain or delegate depends on their personal needs along with the type of rapport with the costume shop.

In some situations, a designer may not be present in the costume shop during the construction phase except for fittings and meetings. A draper or a design assistant may need to decide on behalf of the designer if the designer is not available to answer questions. Texting

Figure 4.9 A complete costume rendering with swatches and research. Renderings courtesy of Anna Buntin.

BOX 4.1 ON COLLABORATION: AN INTERVIEW WITH COSTUMERS LAUREN BRENNAN AND CODY LORICH

Question: What does a typical collaboration look like in the costuming world?

Lauren: Collaboration with the director is what everyone thinks of, but a lot of it comes from the actors themselves. I worked on a show called *The Beaux' Stratagem* by George Farquhar. It's a period piece, but it's so goofy. It's set in the 1700s. All those big, wide skirts called panniers that make your hips like shelves. I designed the mother character—a mad scientist of sorts—to have panniers far bigger than they had any right to be.

Cody: Eighteen inches on each side.

L: Yes! They were big. Because the show was so goofy, my designs were stylistic. I even put syringes in her wig and gave her crazy steampunk goggles—not the period at all, but still fun. But I remember speaking to the actress about what she thought about the character, and if she knew of any fun quirks. The actor said to me, "I think at one point in time, she probably cut off her finger." It was a brilliant idea! So, I gave her gloves that made it look like she was missing a finger. I wouldn't have thought of that if I hadn't talked to the actor.

C: We collaborated with each other a lot, too. Lauren designed the show, I was First Hand. She wanted to make a bodice out of a hoodie. One day, as I was working, I said to Lauren, "Hey, I have an idea. Why don't we make the bustle out of the hoods of many hoodies? Hoods on top of hoods!"

L: It was exactly what I wanted, but I didn't know I wanted it until she asked me. I'm sure Cody gives me most of my good ideas.

C: It's what we always do together. I ask, "What about this? What about that? "and she says, "Yes, that's great!" or "No way!" It's good for a designer to have a healthy relationship with the draper.

Question: What do you do when collaboration fails, or there's a disagreement?

L: Sometimes, you don't know where the communication breakdown happened, especially when you're in the moment. The truth of it is, if things don't work out, I get sad. And that's okay. You should give yourself permission to be sad about it.

C: It's easy to accept disagreement when the final product is better for it. In those situations, I think, "Okay, your solution worked. I was wrong, you were right. It all turned out for the best." But it's harder to reconcile when you have a disagreement, and it doesn't work out as well in the end.

L: You can't get too personally attached to the work.

C: In some cases, the designer doesn't get to make the final call, nor does the director—I learned that from being in professional theater. There are so many times that the producer and the artistic director make decisions that the designer and director didn't initially want. One time, we had this difficult situation at a final dress rehearsal. The artistic director and the playwright came in, looked at the show, and said, "It's not working. We have to change everything." In one day, we changed eight costumes, most of which were garments we built. The designer took the artistic director's note with lots of grace considering the circumstances. We at the shop put in a lot of overtime. At times, we felt defeated, but we did what had to be done.

L: I was once given this vintage designer dress—an original one. It was stunningly beautiful and in excellent condition. I had to recreate it perfectly. I worked two days to do it, working dawn until dusk. It didn't even make it through one rehearsal before the director cut it. I thought, "Are you kidding me? You're not going to at least give it the time of day?" You learn to make peace with the situation, but, man, I find myself grumbling just thinking about it.

C: It hurts when you put a lot of hard work into something and it gets cut. Especially when it's a last-minute thing.

> L: I try to be realistic about these things. My favorite dress got cut in one show I designed. I *loved* that dress. I had ordered a fabric online, but it wasn't what I expected when it came in (the perils of ordering on the internet). It wasn't quite right but time wasn't our side. We went ahead with the build. Because it was the wrong fabric, the dress got cut. It was the right choice. I had to go in and find a new costume. In the end, it worked out great! But I'm sad I ordered the wrong fabric in the first place.
>
> C: The result was fantastic, though.

has improved communication speed; a designer who is away from the shop can share their number with the draper and the shop manager should any essential questions arise. Otherwise, a designer should regularly check emails and answer them promptly.

Some designers are in a costume shop full-time while their show is in production. Depending on their skills, they can assist in costume crafts, stitching, or wigs when they are not shopping, doing fittings, or answering questions. In this situation, a designer has a little more leeway in regards to ambiguous renderings because they are present for all inquiries. However, the more questions that the shop needs to ask, the more time a designer is taken away from required tasks like shopping and pulling.

FABRIC 101

Fabric is a costume designer's primary tool. To execute an effective design, they must know how fabric works, what it does, how it hangs, and what it's made of. The texture and weight of fabric is what characterizes its qualities. A thorough knowledge of fabric will help a costume designer choose the right fabric.

To learn the properties of fabric, first, a designer must learn the way it is created. The most common two types are **knit fabrics** and **woven fabrics**.

The art of knitting is a fabric-making technique that involves two needles looping a single thread of yarn. The origins of knitting are not entirely known. The earliest known example of knitting with two needles came from Egypt. It was a sock dated between the twelfth century CE and the fourteenth century CE (Rutt, 1987). Knitting spread, with different techniques and styles emerging, with mechanized knitting becoming an industry in the nineteenth century (Wilson, Frey).

Woven fabric is created by lining up a series of vertical threads (called a **warp**) on a loom and weaving in a horizontal thread (called a **weft**). The pattern in which a weft is interlaced can create a variety of **weaves**: plain, twill, and satin are all created by varying the way the weft is worked into the warp. This art is thousands of years old with the oldest known evidence of woven fibers dating back 27,000 years (Whitehouse).

The structure of woven fabrics has three "directions": the **selvage**, the **cross-grain**, and **bias**. The selvage edge is parallel to the warp and can be identified by the manufacturer's bound side of the fabric. Garments that are cut parallel to the selvage are considered on grain, which is the strongest direction because it has the least amount of stretch. The cross-grain (or **crosswise grain**) of the fabric is parallel to the weft, perpendicular to the selvage. This direction has a little more stretch. It is considered the ideal grain to go around the curve of the body for a typical garment (with many exceptions—a draper will be knowledgeable in the functions of the grain and when to disregard standard guidelines).

The bias of fabric is on the 45-degree angle from the selvage edge and is the stretchiest direction of the material. This is because there are no fibers to hold the bias into shape when tensile stress is applied. The "box" created by the weaving collapses when pulled, giving bias its defining attributes.

Bias cut fabric can be challenging to sew, but its qualities give garments an elegant drape that hugs the body as it hangs. Madeleine Vionnet popularized bias-cut in the 1920s; her style is still being utilized today.

The fibers used to make fabric (both the knitted kind and the woven kind) come in three categories: **Protein**, **Cellulose**, and **Synthetic**. The composition changes the way it both drapes and how it is dyed.

Protein fibers come from animals, whether it is their fur, their skin, or from worm spit. Common protein fabrics are wool, which typically comes from the hair of sheep, goats, rabbits, and llamas. While these are the most frequently utilized animals, any mammal hair can be made into wool, including human hair. The result would differ in texture, with human hair producing a prickly, wiry fiber that doesn't stick well together (Kroll, 2012).

Wool is good at holding in heat, which makes it an excellent fabric for cold weather. Wools aren't just for cold, though. Different weaves and fibers can create a light, summery fabric. People with sensitive skin may find wool to be itchy when in direct contact.

Silk comes from the spit insect larvae use to create their cocoons, first invented in China. It has a lustrous, smooth texture, but it can vary depending on how the silk is treated once it's woven (Vainker, 2004).

Cellulose fibers come from plants. The most commonly known is cotton. These cellulose fibers grow as a protective barrier for the seeds, called a boll. The bolls are picked either by hand or by machine, then decontaminated of seeds and debris before being spun into yarn.

Linen fabric comes from flax seeds and has been utilized in hot climates like Egypt for its cool, crisp breathable quality. The fiber is also known for wrinkling.

Hemp and bamboo are also common plants used to make fabrics.

Rayon fabrics are newer, invented in 1855 by Georges Audemars as a replacement for silk. Rayon is made from wood pulp and requires extensive chemical treatment to create the fibers for spinning. It can be manufactured to mimic the texture of other natural fabrics, including cotton and wool.

Cellulose fibers are best dyed with fiber reactive dyes, paired with salt and soda ash.

Synthetic fabrics are entirely human-made through chemical synthesis, invented in the late nineteenth century and becoming popular with the mainstream in the twentieth century. Polyester, nylon, and spandex are well-known synthetic fibers.

Polyester and its relatives are also good at waterproofing and avoiding stains. Hikers use the phrase "cotton kills" because cotton absorbs water and holds onto it, losing insulation. But synthetic fibers wick away moisture, protecting the skin against fungal infections and hypothermia. However, synthetics are less comfortable against the skin than a natural fabric. It is also more dangerous to wear near flames. Natural fibers flare. They can be extinguished by "stopping, dropping, and rolling." Synthetics melt and stick to the skin when scalding hot.

All fabrics drape differently depending on the type of fiber and the style of weave. When a designer studies fabric, one should pay attention to the way a garment hangs, then notate the material. Fabric stores sell swatches; each of these can be organized in a binder for reference.

Fabric is sold rolled on a tube or a rectangular piece of cardboard, called a **bolt**. It comes in varying widths, most commonly between thirty-six inches wide and sixty inches wide, though narrower or wider sizes are available. The narrower the fabric, the more a designer needs to purchase. The designer can consult the draper for an exact number for the project. If using a commercial pattern, the recommended amount of fabric is listed on the back of the envelope.

The designer should purchase the fabric far enough in advance for the costume shop to prepare it for cutting. Some fabrics need to be washed as a way to preshrink the fibers and to clean impurities on the surface. Some imperfections may also need to be corrected. When fabrics are rolled onto a bolt, the warp and the weft may become warped. These threads can be reshaped back into place in a process called **blocking**. This can be achieved by steaming or wetting the threads back into place.

DESIGNER PRESENTATIONS

The designers and actors meet as a group for the first time when rehearsals begin. During this initial meeting, the design team shares their vision with the cast and answers any questions that arise. The aesthetic of the show affects how actors approach their characterization. It informs their speech, their movements, and how they interact with each other.

Just as with the final meeting with the designers and the director, the presentation to the actors should be kept succinct, focusing on characterization. The designer can inform the actors about costumes that may restrict movement so that they can practice with rehearsal items. In this presentation, all technical language should be minimized.

More detailed conversations can happen in fittings or with individual meetings arranged with the actor. After the rehearsal, an actor may ask questions in rehearsal reports or emailed to the designer. These should be answered promptly so the actor can continue their work with the correct information. The longer the rehearsal process progresses, the harder it is for an actor to adjust blocking, choreography, and general movements to fit the costume.

REHEARSALS

Rehearsing a show is an organic process. Changes are not only inevitable, they are necessary.

Rehearsals can reveal interesting challenges. As the show develops, a designer can adjust details on costumes to better fit what ideas evolve in rehearsal. This may include adding visual gags to enhance comedies, or to provide accessories to adapt to an actor's character choices. For example, an actor may start to develop nervous behaviors for their character. They may request a watch so they can regularly check the time in a scene. These simple additions can add depth to a character. Designers must adapt to changes and compromise when it is appropriate. Just as the team worked together in the design phase, collaboration continues to be necessary in the production phase.

A designer can anticipate changes by attending rehearsals regularly. Directors and stage managers may not know when revisions affect the costume design. A designer can look for those moments in rehearsals that will not work with the costumes as constructed.

Some common rehearsal changes could include the following: A scene transition may be eliminated, or an actor may stay on stage when they were initially presumed to leave. If the designer plotted a change for the cut moment, the designer should discuss this with the director and stage manager. To solve this problem, the director may add the scene transition back in, or they may cut the costume change altogether. The actor could also change on stage, which may mean altering the costume to be easy to put on without help or a mirror.

An actor may be directed to perform an action that is difficult in the costume as designed. Musicals often require jumps, flips, cartwheels, and leaping over furniture, which can be difficult in normal clothing. If the blocking cannot be changed, the designer and the shop can find ways to make movement easier. Spandex panels in bodices and corsets, plastic boning instead of steel boning, and lighter fabric are all possibilities to help an actor accomplish extreme actions.

Even the way actors stand on stage can provoke design changes. Observe the following hypothetical situation. Three actors wear doublets of different colors: one red, one blue, one green. The director might block the actor wearing red from standing next to the actor wearing green. These colors together for so long may feel too close to the colors associated with Christmas. Were the actors separated, the audience might not make the association, but having them together increases the chances the symbolism connected with the holiday will be noticed. A designer may solve this problem by switching the colors around or eliminating one of the colors.

Significant changes are best addressed early in the process. The later changes come, the more difficult it will be to manage it in a way that will satisfy everyone on the team. Periodically attending rehearsals is the surest way to check for changes.

SUMMARY

- In the costume shop, the designer will work with a costume shop manager, a draper, wardrobe supervisors, and stitchers.
- Depending on the size of the theater, a designer may also work with many costume specialists such as wig makers, dyers, costume craftspeople, and milliners.
- Knowing the basics of garment construction and tools will help a designer better communicate with shop personnel.
- The stage manager compiles reports from rehearsals that record information relevant to the cast and crew.
- Stage managers create the schedule; a designer will request a fitting through the stage manager so that rehearsal time is not impeded.
- Designers can reference measurement sheets for accurate sizing when buying or renting garments.
- The designer can work with the assistant costume designer and the costume shop manager to balance the budget.
- To build the costume, the draper will ask questions regarding construction, research, fabric type, and aesthetic.
- Fabric is made of three types of threads: Protein, cellulose, and synthetic. Those threads can be entwined to create various weaves such as twill and satin.
- Once rehearsals begin, designers will present their ideas to the cast.

5

THE BUILD PROCESS

WHERE TO SHOP?

The biggest advantage of shopping online is the large quantities of clothing available in a range of sizes. It also offers nearly limitless options at prices that seem impossibly low. But all of this variety comes with a need to be cautious. In certain situations, online is not the ideal option over brick-and-mortar stores.

The online store of most major retailers can generally be trusted. If a designer creates an account with a secure password, none but the most common issues (i.e., backorders) should arise. But what if a designer finds the perfect garment on a website that is not well known? What are some ways to confirm a website's reputability?

The first thing one must look for is contact information. A good business prioritizes communication with its patrons, listing the addresses, phone numbers, and emails on their page. Companies that can only be contacted through a text input field should be treated with caution.

When visiting a website, a padlock icon should be pictured before the "https://," indicating a secure connection. In addition, the "s" in "https://" informs the user of a secure connection. Reconsider purchasing from a website that doesn't have both the padlock icon and the "s" in "https://."

The design of the website should feel clean and easy to use. Any messiness, typos, or broken links should be regarded carefully.

A website should have easily accessible customer reviews on their products, though it can be challenging for the average person to discern between legitimate and fabricated reviews. No system is perfect in picking them out, but a typical red flag to look for is a review that sounds too much like marketing speak. Compare the following:

> I love this dress! It looks great, and the fabric feels soft!" versus "Fabric is soft or it's 100% money-back guaranteed. FabriCo has award-winning products that have serviced costumers for over 15 years.

One of these feels like a review written by an actual customer that has bought the product; the latter feels like a marketer wrote it. These types of reviews can be benign, but if the store is compounded by poor website design and an unsecured connection, a designer should be wary before purchasing.

Legitimate reviews can inform a designer about more than just the overall quality of a product. They can give tips and hints about how the garments fit—whether the clothing item is too small for the advertised size, too large, or "fits as expected." They can also comment on the color, quality of construction, and on practical elements that a designer expects: "The pockets aren't real," "the belt is just decorative," or "the dye runs in the wash."

ONLINE SHOPPING CONSIDERATIONS

Online stores come with limitations that may affect the time and budget of a production. Shopping from retail websites can be hit-or-miss because their main product is selling everyday fashion and not theatrical costumes. Finding garments in stores and online that work in a period setting can be difficult. When retailers do sell costume garments, what they offer is usually meant for Halloween or casual use at historical festivals. Designers should research companies and their products so they know what to expect when ordering.

Other points to consider before purchasing online:

You Can't Touch the Fabric

Costumes are a tactile art form. The silhouette may be dependent on the hand of the fabric. Buying fabric that is too light, too heavy, too slick, or too rough will change the character of an outfit. Color may differ from the photograph on the webpage. Even if the retailer took a perfect picture, different monitors have different quality color displays. The true color of the fabric can never be defined unless the actual material is in hand.

Fabric shopping is easier in a bricks-and-mortar store; however, good stores can be hard to find outside major metropolitan areas. If a designer must purchase fabric from an online retailer, ordering swatches is an acceptable substitute. Shipping takes time, so one must plan ahead before a show moves into the shop.

Shipping Costs Money and Takes Time to Arrive

Shipping expenses can quickly add up, especially if a designer relies on expedited shipping. Some retailers, like Amazon, offer free shipping to members, while other websites offer it free on purchases exceeding a specific cost. One can take advantage of these deals to save as much as possible. Shipping costs should be accounted for in the budget.

Mailing packages can take time. In the fast-moving world of entertainment, even two-day shipping may not be quick enough. Online shopping benefits designers that plan. Those that have an ad-lib design style may find themselves delaying fittings to wait on packages. A designer may wait longer for packages that come from a country outside their own due to customs.

The Return Policy Is Too Restrictive

Because store sizes can vary widely between brands, a designer may have to purchase multiple sizes to find the one that fits an actor best. The shop can return the garments not used—usually. Some online stores may have a limited return policy or no return policy at all. If a designer hadn't checked before purchasing, they might find themselves stuck with hundreds of dollars of unwanted merchandise.

Customer Service Is Hard to Contact

If there is a mistake in the order or a designer has questions about the product itself, the best websites have a way to contact the company by both phone and email. Some only have an email, but answer all inquiries within 24 hours. Costume designers have tight deadlines.

Any mistakes in an order can cause detrimental delays. An online store that doesn't offer a method of communication that is quick should be avoided.

BRICK-AND-MORTAR STORES

Physical stores that one can visit in person are known as **brick-and-mortar**. What these stores lack in variety, especially when compared to online, it makes up for in immediacy. Even in major cities with same-day online delivery, going to the local department store can still be faster. In addition to speed, a designer can investigate the garments before they are bought. The sizes can be measured. Returns don't cost shipping.

Just as with online stores, a designer should be familiar with the return policies of brick-and-mortar stores. They may be stricter, often requiring a receipt. Some retailers only give store credit, or they may only allow exchanges for a similar item. Notations can be made in an organizational notebook to keep track of all return policies and deadlines.

For fabric, large cities are the best bet for finding fabric stores. In the United States, New York City, Chicago, and LA host robust garment districts, offering everything from discount trims to exquisite designer textiles. In Europe, Paris, London, Tokyo, Singapore, and Barcelona offer unique stores not found anywhere else in the world. *Joann Fabrics and Crafts* is a major retailer in the United States that sells fundamentals, but it might not have the variety to costume an entire show.

RENTALS

If a shop has no time to build a garment, nor can it be bought, a designer can look into renting a costume from a rental house or another theater.

Depending on the rental house, they may offer different types of costume packages.

A designer may be able to rent a whole show for a flat rate. This works for large commercial musicals that don't have a custom design, using most of the assets from another theater. In these cases, the original designer of the package is paid a licensing fee for their

intellectual property. This option is the cheapest in terms of producing entire shows, but it is the least flexible.

Some rental companies could also charge a set price for one full
costume. Usually, "one costume" is defined by the logical amount of
clothing that would make a complete outfit. That could mean something like breeches, shirt, doublet, jerkin, hose, shoes, and ruff, all
counting under one price.

A rental house may also rent out individual clothing items. Instead
of paying one fee for an entire outfit, the company will charge per
piece. This can be the most expensive rental option, but it is also the
most flexible.

BUDGETING FOR RENTALS

Each rental works with their own pricing structures and policies,
which is important to research as a designer plans the budget. Some
theaters offer their garments for free to educational institutions, as
long as each piece is appropriately dry-cleaned before returning.
Some companies require either full or partial payment upfront, and
some will charge when the show opens.

Rental companies can have service fees that are charged for con-
venience. If the budget allows, a designer can take advantage of these
time-saving opportunities. A designer can have the rental house pull
possibilities based on renderings and measurements the designer
gives them. This cost is a "pulling fee," usually charged per hour. If a
designer has an impending deadline and needs a costume posthaste, a
company will charge a rush fee.

The advantage of organization, especially if costumes are rented
from multiple theaters, is that the designer can document and label
each item appropriately. Usually, this involves photographing the
costumes then recording them in a binder while pinning identifying
labels into the garment. The designer should also check the rental
house's paperwork to make sure everything matches what they have
taken. Once fittings begin, the clothing from the in-house costume
shop stock and the rental's will inevitably mix. If the garments are
neither marked nor adequately documented, it will be challenging to
find everything when it's time to return.

A designer should note any flaws found in a rented garment. If a
significant defect is found, like a tear or rip, the rental house should

be informed as soon as possible. Some theaters will offer a discount if the shop agrees to repair the garment; some may ask for a return.

FITTINGS AND THE ACTOR

A **fitting** is a meeting where the designer, the actor, and the draper try on the costumes and mark them for alteration. Fittings present an opportunity for a costume designer to work out the practical side of their designs. Sometimes, actors bring in new ideas that change the direction of the character. These changes are nothing to fear; it is a natural evolution of the process. The designer can consider the actor's input and either integrate changes to accommodate it or proceed with their ideas as initially intended. Collaboration in the fitting room is just as important as it was with the director.

The way fittings are run depends on the type of theater and the working style of the shop. For a small theater or academic theater, the designer may run a half-hour fitting with just themselves and the actor. At large professional theaters, fittings could be up to 90 minutes with seven or more people in attendance: the designer, draper, first hand, assistant costume designer, costume shop manager, the actor, and sometimes the director. Each of these people has a specific role.

The draper is most familiar with the way a costume fits on the body. A designer will communicate to them how they want an outfit to look (boxy, fitted, tight, baggy, etc.) while the draper pins the garment until it matches the designer's vision. The first hand writes down the fitting notes while supplying the draper with pins, markers, elastic, lacings, or any other material a draper needs. If a first hand is not present, an assistant costume designer or the costume shop manager writes the notes.

The shop manager runs the fitting. They make sure the designer, the draper, and the actor get the information they need. They also keep watch on the clock; actors need to return to rehearsal on time. Without a draper, a costume shop manager may be the one to fit the costumes.

The costume designer guides the fitting. It is up to them to approve the way a garment looks on the body. They may also have a conversation with the actor about practical needs and characterizations discovered during rehearsal.

To prepare for a fitting, the designer and their assistant should set up the room before the actor arrives. This means all costumes, undergarments, shoes, and accessories are laid out and ready to try on. Fittings need to be efficient. A designer that has to run back and forth between the rack and the dressing room wastes valuable time. Depending on the schedule, the costume shop may not get a second chance at a fitting; this is why a designer should prioritize organization.

When an actor arrives, a designer can give a brief overview of what to expect, then provide them with the opportunity to ask questions. After the actor has been on their feet, they may have concerns they need to discuss. To help the actor understand their costume changes, the designer can fit the garments in the order they will be worn in the show. With this information, the actor can visualize what they'll be wearing while they're rehearsing and tailor their movements around the costume's restrictions.

A picture should be taken of each costume, preferably both a front and a back view. This record is useful for three primary purposes.

First, the designer can compile all the photos into a document for easy reference. If ever a designer needs to be reminded about the style or fit of a garment, they can consult the database. For example, if all the members of a chorus need to look the same, the fitting photos can help maintain uniformity.

For a draper, a photo acts as a way to evaluate fit long after the actor returns to rehearsal. Even the most fastidious note-taker will accidentally write an ambiguous note, especially when juggling dozens of fittings. The photo may help decode that note if neither part can remember specific alterations.

Photos help directors visualize how the costumes will look. They can use them to adjust blocking or guide the actor's characterization. A director may give the designer notes on the costumes based on how the show is progressing. New designers may hesitate to show the photos to the director, but if something about the outfit must change, it is better to know earlier in the process rather than later. Not every fitting photo needs sharing; if the picture does not accurately represent the end product (i.e., a garment still in the early stages of construction), it may not be useful to show it to the director. Communication with the director early and often will also build confidence between the two parties.

When working with an actor for the first time, it is necessary to establish trust. One must be open to the actor about what to expect with their costumes and listen to their concerns. For courtesy's sake, a designer should gauge an actor's comfort level before beginning the fitting. Costuming is an intimate art form. The medium in which a designer expresses their art is through the human body. This intimacy, however, comes with responsibility. Just as the technical director oversees safety in the scene shop, so too must designers consider actor safety.

An actor may have body sensitivity issues that can directly impact a costume designer's work. Strong people skills can help the designer talk through the intent of the design so that they both can fulfill the needs of the show. When an actor is on stage, they need to be thinking about their role and not about a costume that bothers or distracts them. The smoothest production process happens when the designer and the actor can reach a mutual understanding about any concerns, ideas, or characterizations.

If an actor expresses concern about a particular part of their body, a designer can talk with the actor about solutions that would make them comfortable. This might mean making a few changes such as adding sleeves, taking in the waist, or lengthening a skirt just enough so that the actor feels secure.

When in a fitting, a designer should frame comments positively, avoiding language that could cause distress. Part of it relies on the designer accurately reading the personality and sensitivity of the actor. Typically, discussion should center on the play and how the costume designer can aid the actor, and how the actor can aid the designer. Comments framed negatively (such as "You look frumpy" or "You have very wide hips") should be avoided, even if the observation relates to the character. Even intended jokes can cause problems. In one situation, a designer had commented that an actor "looked like a grape" in his hat. That touched on an actor's insecurity, which impeded their work. Eventually, the hat was cut from the show. When in doubt, it is best to only use non-judgmental language and to keep conversation professional.

During fittings, ask the actor before engaging in any touching. If the actor says no, respect their decision. If the actor is unwilling or unable to do what is necessary for the costume, the designer should not argue during a fitting. They should request a meeting with the director and production manager to discuss options.

In general, actors are open and receptive to a designer's needs. They know a costume is going to enhance their role in the story-telling. As long as both sides maintain respect for the other's duties, the relationship will be affable and courteous.

DUTIES OF THE COSTUME SHOP

Depending on the nature of a costume designer's contract, they might not be available to work in the costume shop while their show is in production. So, what goes on while a designer is away?

First, the draper studies all the renderings and the research. Once they're confident they know the design, they drape the costumes on a mannequin or draft them on paper. The drapers are one of the first staff in the shop at the beginning of the season.

Once the pattern is complete, a draper passes it off to the first hand to cut the **mockup**, who then passes it to a stitcher to sew. A *mockup* is a test garment, the "first draft" of a pattern using cheap fabric. Depending on the size and the structure of the shop, the draper may sew the mockup themselves.

The costume craftsperson and the dyer will start dying fabric and creating mockup pieces for armor, hats, and accessories. Wigmakers will pattern the actor's heads so that they can begin ventilation. Once this process is complete, they begin the long process of **ventilating**, which describes the intricate knotting of hair strand by strand to create a wig.

On the administrative side, the shop manager will start responding to the stage manager's requests for rehearsal garments and arrange fittings. This is the time for the designer to try on the mockups, rentals, pulled items, and some bought items.

Following the first round of fittings, the shop will begin construction. The first hand or the shop manager will organize a team of stitchers for alterations. The draper will make corrections to the pattern based on the mockups.

A second mockup may be needed for complicated garments, but the time a costume shop is given for construction usually doesn't allow for it. In some situations, the designer may only get one chance to try on the costumes. For this reason, the time used during fittings must be as efficient and informative as possible.

Once the pattern is corrected, the first hand will cut the garment out of the final fabric. During this time, the draper and the first hand will collaborate on the construction method—What kind of interfacing is needed? What kind of closures do they need? Will it be involved in a quick change? Will any special fitting need to be considered? This information is passed on to the stitcher, who starts constructing the garment.

This phase can take a while. Complicated garments could take a hundred hours or more for a stitcher to complete depending on the quality of the construction.

While this is going on, the costume craftsperson will create their foundations from their mockups, then begin details and painting. The wardrobe supervisor will come on board and start attending rehearsals. They will collaborate with the shop manager on the costume changes and assign the tasks for the dressers.

Another round of fittings may begin for those that need it if a show can accommodate another set of requests. Here, a draper will try on the garment in the final fabric, though it may not have all its closures and finishing. This may be the last chance a designer has to try anything on before dress rehearsal.

The shop will then begin on final alterations. Closures and trim will be added to the constructed garments. The wardrobe crew will begin transferring finished costumes to the dressing in preparation for dress and technical rehearsals.

THE ONE-PERSON COSTUME SHOP

Sometimes, a costume designer has no shop personnel to work with. In this situation, they design, fit, stitch, budget, and organize the run. In extreme circumstances, the designer may not be paid for this work. Small theaters that operate on a limited budget usually offer this type of job.

Why might a costumer take a job where they are the only worker? After all, many reputable companies offer both competitive salaries and opportunities to network. It may seem counterintuitive to work a dozen jobs in one. However, there are potential benefits depending on what the designer wants and their life circumstances.

New designers can use this opportunity to build a portfolio. It is challenging to acquire a high paying job with a big company without having the necessary proof that a person can execute competent designs. Very few companies want to give a person of unknown ability thousands of dollars to pull off a complicated costume design. A portfolio is how a designer convinces future employers that they are creative and capable.

Related to portfolio-building is networking. Collaborative art requires a high amount of trust. Getting to know colleagues increases that trust. Favors earn goodwill within the community. When a large amount of money is on the line, companies would rather play it safe and hire people they know rather than take chances on unknowns. This risk-management is why networking is one of the most important skills a designer can develop. One should get to know their colleagues and keep in touch on social media; if they like you, they may call you when they need someone for a job.

A designer may also take a solo-costume shop job because it is a passion project. Directors and designers may make their day job money producing easily sellable mainstream plays for general audiences, but their hearts may want to work on shows that are not as marketable. Sometimes, this leads them to work together to produce shows for low budgets in smaller markets. The limited resources provide a challenge that some designers love to embrace. If the passion is there, a designer should do it.

What about jobs that don't pay? Are the aforementioned reasons still enough to accept the design? A lack of income comes at a cost; not all of them are obvious. If a designer can't support themselves financially, taking on a show without pay could be beyond the realm of possibility. There are compromises a designer makes to help. A designer can take on small design jobs that would allow them the time to have an outside job that pays. With these small jobs, a designer can focus on building a portfolio and networking with colleagues. Some stay with friends or family, if that resource is available. Depending on the size of the show, a designer may not be able to afford to lose that time. The solution is never a simple one; it is a system that plagues artists of all types.

A designer should always be aware of companies that seek to take advantage of their artists. If a theater offers a job without pay, a designer should make sure there is value in the experience. Sometimes, there is no value. Sometimes, a designer will get nothing out of an experience but painful drudgery while the company reaps the benefits from that stress. Designers and the skill they bring should be respected.

How does one determine the line between a company that takes advantage of its workers and one that operates honestly on goodwill? The answer is not always clear, nor are all situations black-and-white. In general, if the costume designer feels respected, if they feel the company appreciates the work they've done, then the experience is valuable. If a company makes a designer feel lesser than others, then perhaps it might not be a good fit.

Some companies may offer a job where the pay is the unused budget for the show. That is, if a show is given a $4000 budget and the designer only spends $3000, then their pay is the remaining $1000. This is not an ideal scenario for either the designer or the theater. With this pay model, the costume designer is incentivized to spend as little money as possible. If they spend all the money on the production, then the designer is left with no pay. A designer should always negotiate a set fee with a separate costume budget.

Working for free is not the only path to becoming a designer. If one cannot afford the means to design for free, other roads can be taken. Networking is an important skill for a designer. Making friends and building professional relationships is an effective way to get opportunities. In any job situation, the key to progressing is to have a good work ethic and to maintain cordial working relationships with one's colleagues.

If a job of this caliber is accepted, the following offers some tips and strategies for success.

If the cast is big and construction time is short, a costume designer should think about simple designs. Simple is not synonymous with bad, and complicated is not the same as good. Simple designs can be elegant and effective, often cutting down unnecessary fluff that is not needed.

When reaching the construction phase, a designer should calculate the number of costumes compared to the time they have to build. Consider the following hypothetical situation:

One person (the designer)
Two weeks
Twenty-five adult actors, 50 child actors, 200 costumes.

There are 336 hours in two weeks. Of those hours, 112 hours are spent on a healthy amount of sleeping. About 56 hours are used for eating. That leaves 168 hours left for labor. With 200 costumes, that's only 0.84 hours worth of work that can be spent on each outfit. That doesn't include hours for self-care, which is also crucial time to budget.

Subtracting that time gives 196 hours left available to work, leaving only 0.98 hours to work on each costume if everything goes according to plan. That includes shopping time, construction time, fitting time, and alteration time.

The size of this type of job would be difficult, but not impossible. Compromises may need to be made. A designer will have to determine if they need to hire a stitcher to help out with their fee. Doing so will free up some time for other needed tasks.

A low budget and limited time don't mean bad or low quality. Limitations can awaken the most creative. Costumers have used coffee filters and doilies from second-hand stores to create Elizabethan ruffs. These are clever solutions to a limited budget that can look great when done right. Having extreme limits forces a designer to think outside the usual strategies.

While good organization paperwork is required in normal design scenarios, it is especially crucial in the one-person costume shop situation. This point is worthy of repeating because it's a step that is tempting to skip. This paperwork will help a designer not forget anything in the weeks leading up to dress rehearsals.

Over the weeks, a designer should pace themselves—slow and efficient wins over fast and careless. Overloading oneself in the first few days will cause a crash later on when the workload builds. In these situations, the designer may be able to ask the cast to provide a base costume that can be built on with pieces. A neutral pair of pants, shoes, and a shirt is the perfect foundation to costume dozens of actors with an extremely low budget. There are many drawbacks to an actor bringing their own costume. With this method, a costume designer loses control over the consistency of the aesthetic. Actors may also forget to bring important items. A designer may also find themselves liable should the actor's personal clothing be lost or damaged. These reasons are why many costume designers prefer this option as a last resort only.

When working on alterations, a costume designer should learn where they can use quick stitching techniques without compromising the aesthetics. It is faster to hem twenty pairs of pants with the invisible hem stitch on a sewing machine versus doing them all by hand. Some styles of alteration can't be skimped. If they are necessary, then the designer should budget the time to complete it. That might mean something else has to be cut to accommodate the workload.

Designers should evaluate whether a job will allow for basic needs, and if it doesn't, it is okay to walk away. Artist culture may encourage all-nighters with people bragging about who slept the shortest. However, the lack of sleep can seriously affect both the quality of the design and the designer's health.

In the journal *Work, Employment, and Society*, Stella Chatzitheochari and Sara Arber of the University of Surrey, Guildford, UK say in their article "Lack of Sleep, Work and the Long Hours Culture: Evidence From the UK Time Use Survey" that sleep loss and fatigue hinders productivity and causes workplace accidents. According to S. R. Price in the article "Sleep Deprivation and Performance," being awake 18 hours is the equivalent of a blood alcohol level equal to 0.05 percent.

To succeed in a job where one person is working all positions, a designer must master time management and organization more than any other skill. There are ways to work around a lack of resources or beginner sewing skills, but nothing can substitute for a well-organized operation. If one never skips the paperwork and always plans three steps ahead, even the most harrowing process can run without incident.

ACTOR'S UNIONS

Actor's Equity is a US union for stage actors that aids in negotiating wages, improving work conditions, and provides benefits like health insurance for its members.

The average contract has a few rules for costume designers and shop managers to follow. What those rules entail depends on the country, region, and size of the theater. To find out what the actors need, a designer can request a copy of the contract from the stage manager. The following section discusses common Actor's Equity requests.

The average contract covers hygiene needs, safety needs, and economic needs. Actor's Equity protects actors from hostile or unsavory work environments, both of which a costume designer could contribute to if they are not mindful of an actor's needs. Following basic rules will earn an actor's trust and respect.

- The costume shop must provide all undergarments unless they are the standard modern style (i.e., boxers, standard bras). This means that if a designer wants to use underwear an actor doesn't typically wear, they can't require the actor to purchase it—the shop must buy it out of their budget. This includes period undergarments such as shifts, corsets, and pantaloons. A costume designer may also need to purchase modern specialty underwear like body shapers or push-up bras.

- Any garment that touches bare skin must be new. An actor should never have to wear an old undershirt that someone else has sweated in previously or a dance belt that another actor has worn. These are necessary considerations for an actor's hygiene. Sweat—and the smell of sweat—can be hard to remove from old garments. Dry cleaning may not be able to remove the faint odor that might linger years after the costume is worn. For courtesy's sake, new underwear is highly advised even for non-equity actors.
- Protective padding must be provided if an actor is asked to do actions that are taxing on the body. If an actor is choreographed to slide across the stage or fall during a fight scene, then they should be given knee pads. However, body-protection is not always in the form of padding. Cooling packs can prevent an actor from overheating in costumes that are heavy and hot. Like the undergarments, the costume shop should purchase brand new protective gear for each actor.
- If a designer wants to use an actor's personal garment or shoes as part of their costume, it must be rented at a price set in an Actor's Equity contract rider.
- Footwear must be sanitary and be in good repair. If the sole is coming off the shoe, it should be repaired with professional quality; if repair is not accessible, a new shoe must be pulled or purchased. If an actor is dancing, then their footwear must be brand new and appropriate to the style of dance. Shoes should also be rubbered, and heels should be reinforced with a brace. This can be difficult for a low budget production. Quality shoes are expensive and can consume a significant percentage of the budget. However, budget issues are not an excuse to compromise an actor's safety. A heel that breaks during a complicated dance can cause serious injury or even death. If proper shoes are too expensive for the show's budget, the costume shop manager can appeal for an increase in budget to accommodate shoe costs.
- All makeup must be provided by the theater, except for conventional street makeup (basic foundation, blush, lip color, and eyeliner). Makeup remover and clean towels must also be supplied.
- Costumes must be cleaned regularly. For undergarments, this means washing after every performance. For days with two

performances, an actor may need a second set of undergarments if the laundry cannot be completed between shows. All garments must be dry by the time an actor is called.

- Wigs and facial hair pieces must be cleaned after each performance.
- Changing an actor's hair color must be agreed upon in writing. If an actor approves the decision to dye their hair, the costume shop must pay for professional dyeing, and then pay to have it dyed back to the original color. This is to protect actors from having to pay $400 or more of their own money to wear a hair color required by someone else. If a designer wants the hair color, they must pay for it out of the budget. If the designer can't afford it, then they should consider wigs as an alternative. Requiring a hair cut beyond a basic trim must also be agreed upon and paid for by costumes.

Equity rules are to protect an actor from being taken advantage of financially or having their safety compromised. Most Actor's Equity rules are easy to follow as long as a designer keeps basic respect in mind for the actors and their job. An actor that feels respected will, in turn, respect a costume designer. A positive relationship between the two creates a more efficient and peaceful work environment.

COMMON CHALLENGES AND WAYS TO APPROACH THEM

No production is ever without its challenges. People are prone to error no matter how much they plan beforehand. If a costume designer can rely on anything, it's that surprises will greet them at each stage of the process. No designer can prepare for every twist and turn that could arise, but they can develop a strong foundation of knowledge to improvise the best solutions.

Costume designers put their heart and soul into their work, and thus, the art by its very nature is personal. But an artist must balance the tricky line between holding one's job close to the heart, but also separating their sense of worth from the work. Criticism is not a comment on the designer as a person. The best problem-solving happens when a designer allows everyone a small sense of ownership in the project, and to not get offended when something doesn't work out. Costume design is both an art and a job; professional decorum is the baseline expectation in all interactions.

In a collaborative art, challenges are faced together. Situations may arise in which the designer may not know the answer, and that's okay. The costume shop, the director, and the design team are there to help. With everyone involved, they can achieve attainable solutions.

The following details common issues that arise in the production process, and some ways to approach it.

The Costume Doesn't Look Right as Designed on an Actor

No matter how good a costume designer is at realistically drawing a character, the transition from a rendering to a garment will often need some amount of design adjustment. The ways a seam is drawn may look great on a fashion plate, but may not flatter an actor's body when they try the costume on. It is reasonable to change details planned on the rendering if it suits the actors better. Changes are not only expected, they're necessary. The design must meet the needs of the show as it evolves. Actors need to feel their clothes match the ideas they have for their character so they may perform to the best of their ability.

If a costume as rendered doesn't look right on an actor, the designer can make any requisite adjustments. The draper can change the general fit, alter the necklines, and move style lines. A designer can ponder whether the fabric choice has the right hand for its intended purpose. Any of these changes should be made as early as possible; once the costume shop constructs the garment out of the final fashion fabric, drastic modification is more difficult, costing the show in both extra labor and money if decisions come too late.

A designer can discuss any corrections with the director and other relevant designers, if only to keep them informed.

The Designer Finds the Perfect Costume for a Character in Stock, but the Garment Can't Be Used

The search for that perfect outfit in a theater's stock can feel like a never-ending scavenger hunt. Through all that searching, a designer may find that one ideal costume, except it might not be the right size for the actor. Or, the garment could be thread-rotted or too fragile to use. If the garment can't be altered, there are a few solutions.

The costume shop can make a reproduction of the garment, but the designer will need to shop for comparable fabric and trim. This solution is less cost effective than altering something from stock, but it can produce the look of the original garment in the size needed. If a recreation of the costume isn't a viable option, the designer can shop or rent something similar. The look might not match exactly what the designer wanted, but dyes, trims, and creative alterations can turn a bought item into the perfect substitute.

The Designer Can't Find the Costume They Want

A script may require a particular costume that's hard to find in stock or in stores. In a theater with a professional shop, the solution would be to add the costume to the build list rather than pull it. But in situations where the designer doesn't have the resources to build the costume from scratch, this can be a challenging puzzle to solve. If the script requires something complicated—for this scenario, let's explore a pink flamingo suit—and the designer has neither the skills nor the money to build one, what can one do?

Renting the costume from another theater is always a possibility. Popularly produced shows might be available in every costume house. The Wizard of Oz, Into the Woods, Little Shop of Horrors are all commonly produced plays and musicals. Their specialty outfits should be easy to find at affordable prices. However, new plays and plays that aren't produced often can return results that come up empty. To approach this problem, the designer should start the plan by listing what they can do rather than focus on what can't be done. Out-of-the-box thinking is necessary.

Instead of searching for a pink flamingo suit, a designer can approximate what the script needs using what already exists. One might take a unitard, dye, trim, and paint it until it's something wonderful. Or one might reinterpret what a "pink flamingo suit" means in terms of the script's themes and only use symbolic motifs to suggest a flamingo which could lead to interesting and creative solutions. A director can be consulted to help brainstorm the difficult elements in a script.

Delayed Shipping

The most difficult trials to overcome are outside the designer's control. A company delaying shipping is one of them. Many situations can cause a package to be delayed indefinitely: caught up in customs, inclement weather, lost in the mail, etc. A designer can make phone calls to confirm shipment, but otherwise, not much can be done to speed up the process, especially if the shop had already paid for a rush delivery.

As soon as a designer finds out their package may not arrive in time, they should immediately organize a backup plan by purchasing from a brick-and-mortar store, pull an alternative from stock, or order from a website that guarantees fast delivery. If the package arrives in time, the designer can return or restock the replacement, but having an alternate costume will keep an actor from having nothing during the first dress rehearsal.

The Show Is Over Budget

Being overbudget is a scary state to be in, but there are strategies one can use to minimize the amount the show runs over by. The first step is to inform the costume shop manager and the production manager about the circumstances and give an estimate on how much more money is needed to complete the show. The designer can also talk with the director about alternative options that better fit the budget. Keeping open communication means that many people can help problem solve together.

The other members of the team may be able to suggest connections that offer free or discounted rentals. Relationships in theater operate on a network. In times of need, a designer can reach out to their network, who can aid in possible solutions.

Conflict Between Personnel

Inevitably, colleagues with clashing personalities will butt heads, but how the designer handles that relationship will determine the productivity and atmosphere of a shop. Because dedication makes good art, a team that is not committed can devastate a project. This means maintaining a professional atmosphere at all times, no matter the conflict. Workers put in more effort for people who make them feel valued. If one must ask for overtime labor, it's easier to agree when there isn't a sourness hanging over the shop. So, what does one do when differences seem irreconcilable?

The best way to handle these relationships is to communicate purely on a professional, business level, leaving personal interactions out of it. The designer can limit conversation to work-related topics only. However, while this strategy works for employees that aren't in constant contact with a designer (like a stitcher or a draper), a strained relationship with the designer's closest associations can be problematic for a production. The relationship between a shop manager, the designer, and the director needs to be symbiotic. The best teams understand each other's process. If a conflict becomes too severe, a designer should report to the company manager or the production manager. Bad behavior should be notated, preferably in an email to the company manager. Email acts as a time stamp should it ever need to be referenced.

The Director Changes Their Mind After They Approve Final Designs

The art of design is an ever-changing, fluid process where flexibility is necessary. What might seem like a good idea early in the process may end up not working once put into practice. Being too rigid in one's ideas can create needless obstacles. When a director requests a change, consider the advice and make the needed changes. However, it is also acceptable for the designer to disagree with the director. Polite discussion or a brainstorming session can help the two parties come to a solution that works for everybody. Neither the director nor the designer should base their decisions on ego—every choice should supplement the story.

If the director is not persuaded, then the designer can either push it (which could damage the relationship if not handled diplomatically) or make the change as requested. Compromise is an important skill for the designer to hone, for it is relevant in all collaborative situations.

Chorus Members Are Added to a Scene During the Rehearsal Process

Even the best-laid plans need adjusted depending on need. Near the beginning of the production process, a designer may receive a document from the director or stage manager that lists every actor's scenes.

Because choruses need to work as a unit, often a designer shops for the garments or fabric at the same time, depending on the show.

Due to the nature of the rehearsal process, chorus members may need to be added or taken out of scenes. A designer can plan for this possibility—if ordering a uniform set of costumes, they can order extra sets in varying sizes. If the costumes aren't ultimately used, they can be returned. If the chorus costumes are to be built, a designer can keep a book of swatches that documents where they bought the fabric and how much per yard it costs. If finding the original garment or the fabric is unavailable, designers can discuss options with the director and the costume shop manager

The Actor Is Injured in the Rehearsal Process

Actors put a lot of stress on their bodies. Inevitably, accidents will happen. The stage manager will keep the costume team informed about the injury—whether it's mild enough that the actor can continue their role or severe enough where they need to drop out. If the actor plans to proceed with the play but with a brace or medical boot, a designer will have to adjust the design to accommodate. With a little creativity, the medical device can either become part of the character's look, or masked with some careful costume placement. The director can help brainstorm ideas.

In the case of an actor dropping out of the production, a designer considers a solution based on the remaining time and budget. First, the draper and costume shop manager evaluate the original costume compared to the new actor's measurements. Sometimes, with a little adjustment and alteration, the show can proceed as planned. But if the new actor's size is different enough from the original actor that the costume won't fit, a designer will have to purchase or pull a facsimile of the original garment. A last-minute replacement of an actor may warrant an increase in the budget which is something the costume shop manager can arrange.

No two shows are ever the same. Inevitably, a problem will arise that no one has ever dealt with before. A designer on any production should remember that they are never in it by themselves. This is the power of collaboration (see Box 5.1)—one must share the art, but everyone together can also share the problems and brainstorm solutions. In theater, no one is ever alone.

BOX 5.1 INTERVIEW WITH CASEY MCNAMARA, JANICE FERGER, AND KATHERINE MCCARTHY

I sat down with three costume shop professionals and asked for their advice about a designer's relationship with the costume shop. Participating in the interview was Casey McNamara, a costume shop manager; Janice Ferger, a draper; and Katherine McCarthy, a first hand.

What is the relationship between the designer and your particular position in the costume shop? How do you like to collaborate with the designer?

Casey: I will say to new people coming to work in the field, knowing that every project is a group project is very important. There's no part about theater that is self-contained. If you have a hard time working with other people, too bad. You need to figure it out or get a new career. When I started, I was not a great people person, but it's a skill I forced myself to learn. And it definitely can be learned! Sometimes there might be specific parts of it that feel too hard to do, but everything can be learned or taught.

Janice: I personally don't like being micromanaged by designers, especially by those who don't know much about sewing. A designer doesn't need to be a professional seamstress, but they need to know enough to have a conversation with me. If they don't know much, they may have trouble communicating what they actually want. And they may end up designing something that is actually impossible to build.

Katie: If you don't have an understanding of physics, please don't design an aqueduct. You need a base knowledge of technique.

J: A designer that knows nothing might end up picking the completely wrong fabric. That's the problem I run into the most. Sometimes, I'll have a designer say, "Oh, this chiffon is the perfect color for this suit!" And I always say, "what? There's no way that's going to look right!" "But the print is perfect!" they say. "It's everything I dreamed!" And then I have to say, "But you're going to hate it."

C: We love when designers ask us for advice.

J: Yes! I don't mind if a designer shows me a rendering and asks me about fabric and construction. I'm happy to give my professional opinion. I can ask things like, "Well, do you want it to have a sheen? Do you want it to float as she moves? Do you want it to be stiff? The rendering looks rigid, so you probably want a heavier weight fabric." It's okay if you don't know. It's my job to help out.

C: The designer needs to trust the costume shop in that we want to put the best product on stage. You should treat them as if you're working with a set of fellow professionals—and that includes everyone from the shop manager to the stitcher—and know that they know what they're doing. Having the shop as a reference point will help you make the most informed decisions. Sometimes a designer might insist on something being light and flowy, but they give us upholstery fabric. It won't give you what you want in terms of silhouette. I've also seen some weird seam lines that make no sense because the designer wouldn't ask questions. It's great to have a stitching baseline, but if you don't, then be okay with that and have the costume shop guide you. The problem comes from when you try to oversee every area because you think a designer designs by controlling every single part rather than letting other people help you fill in the gaps.

K: At it's most basic, you really need to have conversations and problem solve with other people. And you need to know what your primary priorities are to express your design effectively, then be willing to make a decision when you have to make decisions. One of the problems we have with a lot of designers is that they don't want to make the call. And I'm sorry, at the end of the day, it's your responsibility to make the call.

J: My name is just in the program as someone who sewed it, but your name is on the program as the person that conceptualized it.

K: It can be a tricky line to walk between making a decision and consulting other people, but it goes back to Casey's point about trusting the shop. That can be difficult and scary because some shops are better than others, and some are more rigid than others. It's all about learning this new crowd you've just walked into.

J: That can be tough. You walk into a new shop, and you don't know anyone, and you don't know their quality of work other than some pictures you might have seen online.

C: That's why knowing your design is vital because then you know the truth points. If they can't build anything, then you know what to look for online. "I rendered this checkered print neon orange and yellow shirt, and I'll never find it!" So you have to think: is the pattern more important, the color of the shirt, or the style? Knowing what will tell the story best will help you navigate it. One has to be flexible so you know where you can bend and flow and also when to stand your ground. The other thing that is extremely important for a designer is to have some sort of fun or show enthusiasm.

J: Please let us know you like what you're doing. It's definitely work, but we're providing entertainment. If you can't sit back and enjoy what you're doing and let a costume shop enjoy it as well, then it shows in your work.

C: I don't think a lot of costume designers realize that. Because if you are rigid or stressed out, then you create a bad show accidentally. People can't joyously build something if they feel like they're being micromanaged or controlled, or berated for specifics.

J: Or constantly undermined and insulted.

K: I think a lot of it is knowing how to read people. Some people may need a heavier hand. But some may need a lighter hand. Obviously, as a designer, you're working with a lot of different people. And you should like working with people. Sometimes there are people you can't please, but you still have to work with them. I have a lot of respect for people who come up to me and say, "I have a difficult time with people who speak aggressively, and you speak aggressively, so I might struggle to communicate with you." Just having a little bit of humility and telling people about problems so you both can work through them. That will serve people really well.

Speaking of communication and collaboration, how does a designer deal with that? What if a costume gets cut in the middle of tech?

C: First, I would talk to the director about what they don't like specifically because sometimes it might not be about the whole garment. Sometimes, it's just the details that aren't right. Sometimes, attacking those details may give both the designer and the director what they want. Sadly, that's not always the case. If it's a significant component like color that needs to change, then it becomes very tricky. That's a lot harder because of budget and labor. But I will advise a designer to keep calm and reference the shop so everyone can figure out what's doable. Sometimes, if it's a simple garment, it can be built in a short time. But making one too quickly might look horrible, so a designer must consider other options. Also, a designer needs to understand that sometimes the answer is "no, we can't change that."

K: I would also say that having a solid concept as the foundation of your design is incredibly important. With a foundation, you have a point to pivot from.

C: A solid foundation makes the whole design process go easier.

K: It helps a designer think, "What is important to me, and what can I let go of if needed?"

C: Speaking of that too, as a shop manager, I love seeing all the reference photos or a concept board. As a designer, you should realize that not everything has to fall on you. If other people know where you're coming from, they can help.

K: A mistake a lot of young designers make is that they think the design is the thing they're doing, but the concept that supports the storytelling is actually the thing they're doing. The design is just a function of that.

What advice would you give designers about working with actors? What fitting etiquette can you share?

C: I think the best way to start is with communication, and finding out how the shop runs their fittings. A designer should also know how much time they have and gage from there. It's really great for a designer to talk to the actor, but sometimes you don't have the time for that. Sometimes you have a dozen looks to get through in an hour. I think, for me, the biggest thing is knowing how to best utilize the time you're given because it's always less time than you think.

K: Prioritize!

J: As a draper, I will often try to talk with the designer before a fitting about what to expect. In our theater, the draper runs the fitting. In other theaters, the shop manager runs the fittings. Sometimes, they expect the designer to run the fitting. I don't mind if the designer wants to come in and run the fitting. I also don't mind if they expect me to run the fitting. But I do care if they expect me to run the fitting and then interrupt every 30 seconds. Like, either you run it, or I run it, but there's not enough time to battle for charge.

C: Try not to have private conversations with the actors. What might be said in an individual meeting might not make it back to the shop. What is said about costumes must be verbalized to other people so it can be relayed. It's awful when something was promised to an actor, but when it gets to tech, it wasn't done because no one told the shop.

K: An element of that is knowing whose job it is to take notes. You can always approach that person and say, "Hey! Can you write it down that this needs to be taken in?" and I love that. That's what that person is there for. Also be aware that the actor is a human being. Don't yell out bad notes.

J: "Hey! This dress makes her belly look lumpy! Let it out as much as possible! And shop six sizes bigger!" Don't do that! Please don't do that!

C: Never comment on an actor's body in any way, whether positive or negative. Don't assume you're giving them a compliment.

J: We once had an actress in a fitting who said, "Sorry, my hips are weird." And we were like, "No, they seem perfectly normal to us." And she said, "Oh, I had a designer once tell me that my hips were really weirdly shaped, and I would be difficult to costume." We told her they were wrong, and they should not have said that. Clearly, this woman had a complex about this false information.

K: We also had an incredibly self-deprecating actor, and Janice and I were both trying to be as reassuring as possible. Remember that they're human.

C: Knowing as a designer that a costume—as much as they need to fulfill design requirements—they need to have the actor's best interest at heart. The last thing you want is an actor worrying about how they look on stage. And sometimes it's unavoidable. But let them know that it's the garment, it's not you.

K: It's important to remember that the actor also has a job to do, and you shouldn't be an element getting in the way.

J: It helps to be flexible. I'd rather go to a director and say, "You know how I wanted this to be a dropped waist 20s dress? Well, it's unflattering to them, and I'd like to raise the waist because it looks better and will make them look better and serve the story better." Some designers are too married to what they drew on paper to the detriment of the design. If you're unwilling to be flexible, your design might look sloppy. It might look ill-fitting because the shape isn't good for the actor.

C: You're costuming people, not paper dolls.

What would you say to the new designer who takes on a job that is a "one-person costume shop"?

J: I design a lot for theaters that don't have costume shops. I am the entire costume shop in those situations. I only take those jobs when the theater knows what they are. Once, I had a conversation in a production meeting where I asked if they were going to expect wigs because I don't do wigs when I'm the designer. I also wasn't told if there'd be a specific wig designer. And they said, "Goodness no! We're not expecting that."That was good.They knew their limitations. Some theaters don't know. They'll say, "We know you're just one person, but uh, we'd like all these costumes for these fifty children to be built." And that's when you back right out.

C: Knowing how much your time is worth and knowing where you're at in your career is essential. If you're a person who wants to hit the ground running, or if you need credits for your resume, or you'll make useful contacts, then do it. If it's a show you've always wanted to design, then do it, too. Overall, you should know what you want to get out of it, because if you go there and it's just where you're just taking a job for the sake of having a job, then you're probably going to end up hating it.

K: It's also a really thin line between "You have to start somewhere" and "You're being taken advantage of and abused." I think it's practically impossible to describe that line to anyone.

J: And sometimes, you only find that line halfway through an experience. In those cases, you'll learn for next time.

K: Paying your dues is important. But being taken advantage of is something you should be careful of.

C: If it's a terrible situation and you're not getting what you want out of it, honestly, it's never too late to quit. If you have no legal obligation to finish, then walk away from it. There are other opportunities, better opportunities, than letting a company completely abuse you. If you do work for one of these companies, make sure you work out the agreement that you get half the money in advance. If they can't do the full half, then make some financial agreement as a way to prove you will get paid at any point.

J: I worked for a company that said they wouldn't do that, so I said I wouldn't work without it. And they somehow managed it.

C: They need you as much as you need them. You're equal. If they make you feel less than, then they're trying to abuse you. This is the line before you go into a theater.

SUMMARY

- Once the design phase closes and the build process begins, a designer creates organizational documents that will guide themselves and the costume shop through the purchases, rentals, and builds.

- When purchasing, both the online world and brick-and-mortar stores offer seemingly limitless options. Designers can cull their choices by examining a store's viability, including everything from their security to their return policy. Designers that do not find what they need in a store can rent from other theaters.

- After the costumes are gathered together, a designer begins fittings with the actors. Each look is tried on while the designer collaborates with the actor on characterization. In the meantime, the costume shop works on builds and alterations while the wardrobe manager prepares for dress rehearsals.

- In certain circumstances, the costume designer will be a one-person costume shop who plays all the roles in one. These designers must master organization and time management to adequately pull off a quality product while maintaining their health.

6

TECH, DRESS, AND OPENING NIGHT

WHAT IS TECH?

Technical rehearsals (or "tech") begins the final stage of the production process. During these rehearsals, the team troubleshoots all the technological and production elements.

Preceding tech, actors work on a facsimile of a set, with the ground plan taped out on the floor with odd items standing in for furniture and props. But in tech, actors rehearse on the completed set for the first time, using staircases, doors, and props. The lighting designer hones their lights and adjusts the colors to best accent the stage and actors. Sound balances the levels of the speakers, then adjusts the microphones on the actors. The **deck crew** practices the intricate choreography of scenic changes, moving **wagons** and furniture so efficiently, the audience barely notices their movements. The stage manager practices calling the show, which is a rhythmic set of instructions based on dialogue, action, music or dance called through a headset during the show. These instructions cue the **board operators** and the deck crew to take specific actions at a precisely timed spot in the show.

Depending on the mechanical challenges, tech can be a week long, a month long, or five months long. Where the tech process begins depends on how a theater structures the rehearsals. Costumes may or may not be a part of tech, depending on the theater's typical rehearsal schedule. Some theaters may elect to tech scenic transitions and work light cues before introducing costumes, while others like to work set, lighting, sound, and costumes together. If a costume designer has a preference, they may discuss options with the production manager, director, design team, and costume shop to work out the best schedule for the show's needs.

TYPES OF TECH REHEARSALS

When a production manager (or stage manager) sends out the tech schedule, they may include specific types of rehearsals. Each has a specific purpose designed to maximize productivity for as many people as possible. The following are a few types of rehearsals a designer will encounter.

Dress Rehearsals

Dress rehearsals make up the final stage of the production process. Typically scheduled for three rehearsal days leading up to preview, a dress rehearsal's purpose is to fine-tune the costumes while practicing the changes. The ideal dress rehearsal runs the show start to finish without stopping save for mistakes or hazards.

Tech/Dress

A tech/dress rehearsal is a combination of the two types of rehearsals. Actors wear costumes, though they do not run the show start to finish. They step through the show minute by minute in a rehearsal called a cue-to-cue. In cue-to-cue, the lighting and sound designers evaluate each moment and adjust the lights so that the actors are properly lit and the mood matches the scene. Tech/dresses are long, but they are critical for a successful run.

Cue-to-Cue

A *cue-to-cue* is a process that allows the stage manager and the lighting designer to refine their work by taking the show one step at a time. Cue-to-cues are a slow process, sometimes only covering small portions of the script of the course of a workday. These steady, measured steps, however, are critical to a smoothly run process once the show begins to run in real time.

If costumes are worn during cue-to-cue, the slow pace helps the actors grow accustomed to their garments before they have to wear them during a run. During tech, the wardrobe crew may not be able to practice the quick changes in real time. If the show has an actor change that may prove challenging, the designer can make a request to set aside rehearsal time to run the quick change.

10-out-of-12

A 10-out-of-12 describes the longest rehearsal day during Tech. It means that the rehearsal runs twelve hours with a two-hour meal break for the actors. The wardrobe crew sometimes arrives hours before to set up the dressing rooms before the actor's arrival, and leaves hours after, once the crew completes the laundry. The number of 10-out-of-12s a theater can schedule depends on an Actor's Equity contract.

7-out-of-9

A rehearsal that works on the same principal as a 10-out-of-12, a 7-out-of-9 describes a period where the actors work seven hours out of a total of nine hours.

THE TIMELINE OF TECH/DRESS

The Days Prior to Tech/Dress

The days leading up to technical rehearsals are a busy time for the costume shop. The final push can involve long hours getting all the details ready for the actors. Smaller costume shops may have to prioritize what is called "**fit-and-function**" notes. "Fit-and-function" is a term used to reference the construction notes needed to make the garment wearable and safe (i.e., buttons, snaps, zippers, hems) as opposed to notes that are only aesthetic.

The designer, along with the wardrobe supervisor and the costume shop manager, compares the piece list and alteration notes with the garments on the rack ready for the dress rehearsal. This is the last chance to address missing items. If the designer waits beyond this point, the actors may not have what they need during tech/dress. While switching out minor details like socks or undershirts usually is not a problem for an actor, giving them major pieces of the costume after the first or second dress rehearsal can disrupt their work. However, circumstances may make it necessary to introduce new elements late in the process. Sometimes, a costume does not work out but good organization can minimize needless changes.

This is the stage when the wardrobe supervisor studies the piece list and the costume plot, then creates a run plot in collaboration with the designer. A **run plot** is a set of instructions for the dressers that coordinates their movements to maximize the efficiency of scene changes.

Before technical rehearsals begin, the director may host a special rehearsal called a **crew view** for the stagehands, board operators, and dressers who may never see the show from the audience's perspective. Crew views help the deck crew understand the story's pacing and their role in it. This is an opportunity for the designer and the wardrobe supervisor to inform the crew about the tasks and potential challenges they are about to face.

In theaters with a tightly compacted rehearsal schedule, there may not be the time for a crew view. Dressers may have to go into a production without ever having seen the show, which means well-organized paperwork from the designer is crucial. A piece list that is not up-to-date may cause the dressers to search for garments that don't exist.

A director may request an event known as a **dress parade**. In dress parades, the actors present their costumes to the director in a procession before technical rehearsals begin. There are pros and cons to dress parades. One advantage is that it helps the director get a clear visual of the show, especially if they have a difficult time interpreting renderings. Another advantage is that the actor gets experience putting on their costume, especially if the garments are atypical.

Some designers reject dress parades, because the cons for them outweigh benefits. The audience will never see the costumes out of context with the lights and the set, akin to judging an entire painting by isolating the figures. Costume designers can't take notes on color and aesthetics without the other elements present. Only fit notes will be relevant.

With the costume shop finishing last notes and the wardrobe run crew choreographing their actions during the run, tech/dress rehearsals begin.

The Morning of Tech/Dress Rehearsal

Dress rehearsal is the culmination of the costume department's planning and work. This is the day the costume designer gets to see all their work in the context of sets and lights. The goal of the crew is to run the show as smoothly as possible so that the designer can focus on refining the costumes rather than fixing major mistakes.

On the morning of the first dress rehearsal, the wardrobe supervisor is the first to arrive, followed by the dressers. If the show requires a wig crew and makeup team, they would arrive at the same time, though the exact times vary depending on the situation.

By this point, the dressers should intimately know the play and their run plot for the actors they are assigned to assist.

This team arranges every costume piece—from the socks, to the large gowns, to the smallest ring—and places them in their proper dressing room in an order that makes sense to the actors. They organize the wigs in neat rows with labels and prep the necessary makeup. If any character has specialty makeup or prosthetics, that crew will start applying on that particular actor hours before the others arrive.

In a world where everything goes as planned, all costume construction, trims, and details are completed by first dress. But precarious circumstances can be hard to predict. When something goes wrong, not every item may make it to first dress rehearsal. This is considered a less-than-ideal situation, because the shop removes a day for the actor to acclimatize to their costume. Should time be tight in the days leading up to dress rehearsal, and it becomes evident that some costumes won't be completely done by first dress, a shop can try the previously mentioned fit-and-function notes over trim and aesthetic notes. Dress rehearsal is as much for the actor as it is for the costume designer, and it is important for them to be able to work the show wearing their costume, especially if it fits differently than the average modern-day outfit.

For a designer managing their own shop, the best strategy for dress rehearsal is to minimize the amount of unfinished notes as much as possible, even aesthetic ones. During the run, costumes might break, garments may not work out, quick changes may need to be refined. Dress rehearsals present a litany of its own notes on top of the previously unfinished ones. In this case, it will be difficult for the shop to finish everything. Proper time management begets a smooth dress rehearsal.

The actors can arrive anywhere from an hour before *go* ("Go" describing the time that a show is set to begin) to a half hour before. Equity actors are always called a half hour before *go*, with a few exceptions, like those that need specialty makeup. During this time, the wardrobe crew will assist the actors into their costume pieces—lacing corsets, putting on wigs, adjusting ties, clearing coats of lint with a roller. The actors will likely have many questions on first dress. While the wardrobe supervisor will be able to answer some of them, the designer should be present near the dressing room for complicated questions.

30 Minutes Before Go

Some actors may not have the full half-hour before *go* to focus on dressing. Depending on the type of show, the actors and some of the backstage crew may need to complete two major tasks before the tech rehearsal begins.

One is called **fight call**, which is a drill set aside for the actors to practice any scene that involves intense physical contact. Stage combat can cause serious injury if not executed perfectly. Fight call gives the actors an opportunity to rehearse that moment so that when it comes up during the run, the actor feels prepared. The stage manager may request that the actors are in their costumes for fight call.

The second task is called **mic check**, a scheduled period where actors walk on stage with their microphones attached to them and speak lines from the show (or sing if it is a musical). The sound board operator uses this moment to set appropriate levels.

If a show has neither a fight in it nor uses microphones, neither of these events take place.

The First Full Dress Rehearsal Run

When cue-to-cue ends, the team begins a full run of the show, only stopping if a technical or blocking problem arises. This is the first time a designer sees their costumes as they are meant to be seen in the show, with all the actions, lights, choreography, moving scenery, dialogue, fights, sound, props, projections, story pacing, and music working together to tell the story.

If the costumes were worn during tech, then the notes at this point should be centered on refining the aesthetic. If the run is the first time the costumes are seen on stage, then the designer will take notes on four fundamental categories: aesthetics, fit, practical notes, and actor-specific.

BOX 6.1 TYPES OF NOTES AND WHAT TO LOOK FOR

AESTHETICS

Aesthetic notes relate to the way the costumes look in context with the sets, lighting, sound, projections, blocking, and choreography. If a designer has a firm grasp of their concept, they should be able to see if its execution has translated properly to the stage. For example, if a costume was meant to portray a specific idea or theme like loneliness, but the actor's blocking, the bright lights, or the colorful set make the costume look more cheerful than was intended, the designer can contemplate ways to alter the color, trim, and style to emphasize the original idea. The solution could be as simple as adding trim or complicated as pulling an entirely new costume.

Audience perspective can also change the way a costume is regarded. The farther the actors from the audience, the less they can perceive the individual features. If a detail is lost, a designer can use a few techniques that emphasize details.

The same color theory rules that worked for the costume renderings also work for the stage. Low contrast colors fade together, high contrast stands apart. A designer can add highlights and shadows with trim, dye, or paint to emphasize details. Luminous trims can be subtly added to elements that need to draw the eye.

One can also brainstorm ideas with the lighting designer, especially if the costume designer's color choices and the lighting designer's choices clash. A designer should not demand changes, but, just as with the other stages in the production process, collaboration may reveal a creative solution.

FIT

Human bodies vary depending on numerous variables, many of which can't be predicted. What worked in fittings might not be working in dress rehearsal. As the actors progress through their blocking and choreography, a designer can look for garments that don't fit quite right or don't move like they need to move. Hems might look too long or too short, pants may be too tight or too loose, a skirt may not flow quite as intended. The designer can take notes based on how the garment is fitting, and consult with the draper and shop manager about solutions.

PRACTICAL NOTES

These notes are for the actor's ability to function in the garment. To recall back to the design phase, the designer likely considered the accuracy of historical garments, and whether to take liberties or to portray it authentically. Dress rehearsal reveals the practical side of that design choice. Period garments made as they were in history may not be conducive to the movements an actor needs to play their character. If an actor struggles with their costume, a designer can take action to aid them.

If the arm cannot move in the sleeve as constructed, a designer can add a **gusset,** which is a fabric shaped like a football stitched to the underarm seam. This additional fabric allows more movement to fitted sleeves. If hats fall off, the shop can add straps, loops, or adjust the structure to help the fit. Actors may need to store props in pockets the designer must hide strategically. These are covert methods meant to maintain a show's fluidity and sense of pacing, preserving a story's momentum.

Quick changes are a common practical note. If a change seems faster than originally predicted, a costume shop can rig a garment with hardware-like snaps or zippers to aid the dressers. In some instances, a designer may discover a quick change that is faster than what traditional methods can accomplish, oftentimes requiring a near-instantaneous transformation. Over decades, professional magicians have perfected the instant-costume-change. Many have written books revealing their secrets, which a costume designer can use. Magnets achieve speed, but they can stick to one another if the dressers aren't careful laying out the costume. A shop can also rig costumes with fishing line and loops that, when pulled, cause costumes to fall off the body, revealing another costume underneath.

ACTOR OR DRESSER NOTES

When an actor wears a hat backwards, puts on the wrong tie, or the dresser forgot the wig in the quick change, the designer will take an actor/dresser note. These are not meant for the costume shop, but the wardrobe supervisor, who will relay the note and reorganize as necessary.

Backstage, the wardrobe crew performs intricate choreography of their own. Each member will know—or come to know—each beat of the performance and move precisely to where they are needed and when they are needed. A dressers' work is intricately timed, helping the characters' changes flow naturally through the story.

Each dresser must anticipate their actors' changes and prepare a small area for the moment, laying out each costume piece in an order that helps dress the actor the fastest. Once a quick change begins, the actor will run off stage, dropping pieces of their current costume while the dressers put on the new costume. When the quick change is completed and the actor has returned to the stage, the dressers retrieve the discarded garments and return them to the dressing rooms.

At the end of the dress rehearsal run and the actors taking their bows, the director can choose to rehearse specific scenes depending on the time left available in the day. Afterwards, the actors are dismissed for the day. As they change out of the costume, the director and the design team begin tech notes.

Tech Notes

At the end of the day, all the designers and the department heads gather to talk about concerns, notes, and strategies for the next day with the director, though the exact topics depend on the theater.

Some commonly discussed notes might include how the shoes interact with the set, how hats might cast a shadow that lighting can't reach, or how actor movement might alter based on the fit of the costume. Tech notes are the time to discuss those problems so the team can work on solutions together.

Afterward

As the actors get out of costume, the wardrobe crew returns all the costumes back to the proper place on the rack, spraying each down with a wardrobe spray made up of a mixture of high-proof vodka and water. The alcohol in the vodka kills the bacteria that cause body odor, which aids in the cleaning of garments that can't be laundered in a machine. For spaces that don't allow alcohol, commercially available cleaners can act as a substitute. Fragrance-free detergent and sprays tend to be preferred to prevent possible skin irritation on the actors.

With all the costumes washed, pressed, steamed, repaired, and hung up, the costume shop closes and prepares for the next day of tech.

The Day After

The mornings after a 10-out-of-12 are reserved for each tech department to work. The designer and the costume shop manager compile their notes into a list.

The shop needs to complete as many as possible before the wardrobe crew begins their pre-show check-in. Like the days before tech/dress, the fit-and-function notes are best prioritized if there isn't enough time to finish everything. Pieces missing in the first dress must be present for the second dress. The lighting designer should be informed immediately of any major costume color changes.

Dark Day

The term "dark day" refers to a night off for the actors and the run crew, so called because the theater lights are not turned on that day. Theater technicians use this day to catch up on notes and work on projects that might need multiple days to complete, like painting and dyeing.

2nd Dress and Beyond

The process is repeated for the remaining dress rehearsals, with the notes each day becoming more and more detailed and refined. It is unlikely that major changes will happen at this stage, but there are some circumstances where a costume just doesn't work despite tweaks and adjustments. In these situations, the costume shop manager will help determine the feasibility of a last-minute change, and the labor strategy required to pull it off.

Invited Dress and Previews

The presence of an audience changes the energy and dynamic of a show. The sooner the actors can practice in front of people, the more prepared they will be to react accordingly on opening night. An invited dress traditionally falls on the last dress rehearsal before previews. It is an event where people can come by invitation only— usually the family and friends of the production staff. This audience can be very small, but it is sufficient enough to communicate to the actors where laughter might be in the story and with whom they can interact if the show has audience participation. This rehearsal is run like a normal tech night.

After invited dress comes previews, which are dress rehearsals with a ticketed audience. A stage manager calls no holds in a preview unless emergency situations arise. The audience member pays a reduced price with the foreknowledge that the show they're seeing is still in rehearsal. While the show should be polished by this point, the director or stage manager can still pause the show to work a moment if needed.

Previews can run from a single day to several months, depending on the complexity of the technical elements. Some theaters choose not to run a preview at all. Official reviews of the show don't happen until opening, but word of mouth can still spread, giving the theater that kind of marketing before opening night.

OPENING NIGHT AND THE POST-MORTEM

While opening night is only the beginning for the cast and crew, it is "The End" for the design team—the completion of their contract.

Opening is a time of celebration where family, friends, cast, and crew come together to commemorate the thousands of hours of labor among dozens of people to create a story that people will come to enjoy. Nothing can change after opening; the costumes, choreography, set, blocking is all "frozen" until the end of the run, to maintain the integrity of the show for every audience.

With the designer's contract ended, the costume shop manager and the wardrobe supervisor maintain the integrity of the show. They may contact the designer again if an emergency happens, but, typically, a designer has little involvement after opening, with the exception that the designer is a resident of the company or is a one-person costume shop.

Any artist that worked on the production can fixate on what could have been and how things might have gone better, which is good for self-evaluation, but one must also stop and rejoice in the accomplishment before moving on to the next project. Afterwards is a time for reflection, especially for student and early professional designers. If needed, a production manager can schedule a special meeting called a post-mortem. Post-mortems are a formal discussion where one can discuss a project's successes and failures. Problems solved in the moment may result from quick-thinking and adrenaline, but hindsight provides the opportunity to brainstorm better solutions for the future. A costume designer can ask themselves the following questions.

Was I satisfied with the ultimate look?
What would I do different had I the chance to do it again?
Did the production process go smoothly? If not, what went wrong and how can it be troubleshooted?

This self-evaluation will help mollify complications on a show in production, leaving more room for designing.

When the run ends, the costume crew initiates the final phase of a theatrical show: **Strike**. Strike is the deconstruction of a show to prepare the stage and the shops for the next show—the dressers and shop manager launder, restock, repair, restore, and return the rentals while cleaning the dressing rooms. Once strike is complete, the show is gone, existing only in videos, photographs, and memories.

And that's the conclusion of a show's lifecycle. The next show begins the process all over again, in perpetuity, as long as the designer is willing and able to do their craft.

While the fundamental steps of production remain the same, no two shows are interchangeable. The appeal of costume design as a career is that it constantly surprises, bringing new challenges every day. Stories affect people—their emotions and their thoughts. Such a thing can't happen without people bringing the characters to life.

SUMMARY

- Tech and dress are rehearsals dedicated to working the mechanical elements of a show. Usually scheduled during the weeks leading up to opening night, dress rehearsals are the first time a costume designer sees everything in context with the other designers' work.
- Opening night marks the final day of a designer's contract. Once the costume designer moves on to the next project, the costume shop manager and the wardrobe crew maintain the integrity of the show during the run. At the end, the crew strikes the show and the shop prepares for their next production.

VOCABULARY

achromatic Colors that do not have a hue; neutral colors such as black, white, and gray. Mixing a chromatic color with an achromatic color changes only the tint or shade, not the hue.

additive mixing The process of mixing light. Photons are added together to make white.

analogous Color adjacent to each other on the color wheel.

antagonist The force that opposes the protagonist that can come in the form of a human, nature, society, or the protagonist themselves.

bias The direction of fabric 45 degrees from the selvage. The bias is the stretchiest part of the material.

blocking How the actors are staged in a play.

board operators Stage crew in charge of a computer that executes the lights, sounds, and projections during a show.

bolt A large yardage of fabric stored on a roll or cardboard square.

brick-and-mortar store A physical store that sells goods and services.

caricature A distorted representation of a person.

cheat sheet An abridged version of the measurement sheet.

CMYK Cyan, magenta, yellow, and black: The primary colors used in printers in addition to black.

color palette A collection of colors that makes up the design's overall scheme. A palette is also a hardboard that painters use to mix paint.

color wheel A drawing that depicts the visual spectrum of light in a wheel shape. Relationships between colors can be determined based on their placement on the wheel.

complementary Colors on opposite sides of the wheel.

concept A show's mood, tone, setting, and aesthetic.

costume plot A document that charts the number of costumes, which character wears the costume, and when they are worn in the show.

costume rendering A drawing or plan that represents what the costume design will look like on stage.

contrast Highlighting the differences between colors based on their comparison.

crew view A rehearsal that allows the deck crew to see the show from the audience's perspective.

croquis A quick drawing of a live model.

cross grain (or crosswise grain) A direction of fabric that runs perpendicular to the selvage; the direction of the weft.

cut The *cut* of a garment refers to the way the garment's shape is achieved through the cutting of the fabric.

cutting The act of placing pattern pieces on fabric and cutting. Cutters must be experts in pattern matching and arranging perfect grain lines.

dance Movement based theater based on the manipulation of the body to music.

deck crew People tasked with managing the backstage and the scene changes during the run of a show.

designer A person who devises the look of a show or film according to their area of discipline.

- **costume designer** Creates the look of the characters.
- **lighting designer** Creates mood and atmosphere using light to sculpt the scene.
- **scenic designer** Devises the environments in the story.
- **sound designer** Creates mood and atmosphere using soundscapes and music.

designer run A rehearsal where all designers are invited to see a nearly finished play. These are called when the director is confident that the blocking won't change much. Lighting designers use it to determine an actor's placement so the lights can be focused. Set designers use it to note how, when, and where the actors use the set and props. Costume designers use it to watch for quick change timing and for unexpected movements that could affect wardrobe choices.

devised theater A story created by a group through rehearsals and workshops.

director The person in charge of interpreting the script and creating a cohesive vision on stage or on film. The designers and actors answer to the director.

dramaturg A position in theater that specializes in research, and assists with playwrights, rehearsals, and production by giving context to the creative team.

dress parade An event that showcases costumes in a procession.

dress rehearsals A set of rehearsals toward the end of the production process where costumes are introduced on stage with the sets, lights, and actors.

extant garment A piece of clothing that has survived time.

fight call A short rehearsal scheduled before a run that allows the actors to practice difficult and dangerous moments in the play.

fit-and-function Costume notes that affect how a garment fits on an actor as opposed to aesthetic notes, which only affect how the garment looks.

fitting A block of time reserved to try costumes on an actor.

framing How an author wants the audience or readers to feel about the characters and the story.

French scenes Scenes that are divided by the exits and entrances of the characters.

hand (of the fabric) The weight of a cloth and how it drapes.

high waist (empire waist) A waistline that sits just below the bust.

hue Another word for color.

improv Short for improvisation. A type of show where the performance is created on the spot from a prompt.

inseam A measurement on the inside of the leg from the crotch to the ankle.

low waist A waistline that sits along the hip bone.

measurement sheet A catalog of the actor's measurements.

metaphor The use of a symbol or figurative language to represent an idea or articulate a point.

mic check A block of time scheduled before each show where the sound board operator adjusts the level of an actor's microphone.

mockup A trial garment made from cheap material like muslin.

natural waist A part of the body just below the ribcage where the torso bends.

paratext Supplemental material to the text including blurbs, forewords, footnotes, author blogs, notes from the editor, or social media posts.

patterns A flat diagram that is used as instruction for creating a wearable costume.

piece list Paperwork that lists all items an actor wears.

preset To place a garment in a convenient place for a costume change that happens offstage rather than in the dressing room.

primary colors The foundational colors from which all other colors are made.

primary research Documentation of a period as it was lived; first-hand accounts in the form of photographs or diaries.

production schedule A calendar of all the significant events during the production of a show, including design meetings, photo calls, and rehearsals.

protagonist The character that is the driving force of a story.

quick-change plot A document that lists the scenes where an actor needs to change costumes in under a minute.

rehearsal report A document that records rehearsal information relevant to the cast, crew, production team, and designers.

RGB Red, green, blue, the primary colors of light.

rise On a pair of trousers, a rise describes the distance between the crotch and the waist.

run plot Paperwork that plots the dresser's actions during a show.

RYB Red, yellow, blue: The primary colors for pigment.

saturation The level of a color's neutrality.

script The written dialogue and stage directions that make up a play or story. It is the reference material for the actors and the production crew to create a show or film.

secondary colors Colors made by mixing primary colors.

secondary research An analysis or an interpretation of an event written or composed after the event happened. Newspaper articles, historical blogs, and textbooks are secondary research.

selvage The bound edge of the fabric parallel to the warp. Patterns placed along this line are considered on grain.

shade A color with black added.

shorthand Visual clues that impart information to an audience quickly.

silhouette   The general shape of a garment indicative of its time period.

stage manager   A position in theater to record notes, write reports, schedule and run rehearsals, organize techs, and call shows. A liaison between the design and directing team and the actors.

stock   A collection of costume items from previous shows and donations that can be used to augment a designer's current project.

strike   An event upon completion of the run where the deck crew tears down the set and the wardrobe crew launders, restocks, restores, and returns all costumes.

stumble-through   The earliest run-through. The actors run through the show start to finish, but the blocking may still need to be adjusted, and lines may still need to be called. Stumble-throughs are the equivalent of a show's first draft.

subtext   A theme or message implied by the text, but not directly stated.

subtractive mixing   The process of mixing pigments. It is subtractive because mixing takes wavelengths of light away from white.

subversion   To play against an audience's expectations.

suspension of disbelief   The level of which an audience is willing to accept a story as real.

temperature   A color's warmth or coolness. Warm colors are in the red, orange, and yellow range. Cool colors are in the green, blue, and violet range.

tertiary colors   Colors made by mixing a primary color and a secondary color.

tertiary research   A collection or compilation of primary and secondary sources; almanacs, dictionaries, and encyclopedias are types of tertiary research.

theme   The central idea or subject matter addressed by a script.

tint   A color with white added.

trope   A device commonly used across all fiction, used as shorthand to communicate an idea quickly.

value   The lightness or darkness of a color.

vanity sizing   A marketing technique that assigns smaller numbers to the sizing of clothes as a sales tactic.

ventilate A wig-making technique where each hair is individually tied with a small latch hook.

verisimilitude A plausible portrayal of reality; suspension of disbelief.

wagons Scenery mounted on castors so that it can move around the stage.

BIBLIOGRAPHY

Abumrad, Jad and Robert Krulwich. "Colors." Audio blog post. Radiolab. WNYC studios, 21 May 2012.

Anderson, Donald M. *Elements of Design*. Holt, Rinehart and Winston; Geelan, 1961.

Bevington, David. "Much Ado About Nothing." *Encyclopædia Britannica*, 20 November 2019, www.britannica.com/topic/Much-Ado-About-Nothing-by-Shakespeare

Coffin, Sarah et al. *Rococo: The Continuing Curve, 1730–2008*. Cooper-Hewitt, National Design Museum, 2008.

Color: Color Theory and Color and Light. Dir. David Brody. The Great Courses, 2015. Kanopy. Web. 17 July 2019.

"Dates and Sources: Much Ado About Nothing." *Royal Shakespeare Company*, 30 June 2013, www.rsc.org.uk/much-ado-about-nothing/about-the-play/dates-and-sources

Finlay, Victoria. *Color: a Natural History of the Palette*. Random House, 2004.

Font, Lourdes. "1963 – Mankiewicz, Cleopatra." *Fashion History Timeline*, 27 August 2017, fashionhistory.fitnyc.edu/1963-mankiewicz-cleopatra/

Gintert, Kristin. "Can You Make Yarn out of Human Hair?" *Happiness Is Handmade*, 6 March 2019, www.howtoarmknit.com/can-you-make-yarn-out-of-human-hair/.

Herman, Eleanor. *The Royal Art of Poison: Fatal Cosmetics, Deadly Medicines, and Murder Most Foul*. Duckworth, 2019.

Kay, Dennis. *William Shakespeare: His Life and Times*. Technical Publications, 1995.

"Knitting's Early History" 16 March 2016. Stuff Media LLC. www.missedinhistory.com/podcasts/knittings-early-history.htm

Landis, Deborah Nadoolman. *Screencraft – Costume Design*. Focal Press, 2003.

Landis, Deborah Nadoolman. *Dressed: A Century of Hollywood Costume Design*. Collins, 2007.

Lauer, David A. *Design Basics*. Holt, Rinehart and Winston, 1990.

Price, S. R. "Sleep Deprivation and Performance." *Anaesthesia*, vol. 58, no. 12, 2003, pp. 1238–1239. doi:10.1046/j.1365-2044.2003.03534.x.

Rutt, Richard. *A History of Hand Knitting*. B. T. Batsford Ltd., 1987.

Sorabella, Jean. "Portraiture in Renaissance and Baroque Europe." In Heilbrunn Timeline of Art History. New York: The Metropolitan Museum of Art, 2000–. www.metmuseum.org/toah/hd/port/hd_port.htm

Sutton, Peter C. *Northern European Paintings in the Philadelphia Museum of Art*. Philadelphia Museum of Art, 2000.

Tanner, Tony. *Prefaces to Shakespeare*. Belknap Press of Harvard University Press, 2010.

Wikipedia contributors. "Rococo." Wikipedia, 7 October 2019.

Wilson, Kax. *A History of Textiles*. Westview Press, 1979.

INDEX

Note: Page numbers in *italic* refer to figures in the text.